# BRUNCH
# KING

# BRUNCH KING

—•— A COOKBOOK —•—

## EATS, BEATS, *and* BOOZY DRINKS

## JOEY MAGGIORE

PHOTOGRAPHY BY JOANIE SIMON

**Figure.1**
*Vancouver / Toronto / Berkeley*

*To my father, Chef Tomaso, for passing
on your passion for life and cooking to me;*

Recipes are chef tested.

24 25 26 27 28 5 4 3 2 1



Cataloguing data is available from Library and Archives Canada

ISBN 978-1-77327-235-1 (hbk.)

Design by Teresa Bubela
Photography by Joanie Simon
Food styling by Ellen Straine

Editing by Michelle Meade
Copy editing and proofreading by Marnie Lamb
Indexing by Iva Cheung

Printed and bound in China by C&C Offset Printing Co.

Figure 1 Publishing Inc.
Vancouver BC Canada
www.figure1publishing.com

Figure 1 Publishing is located in the traditional, unceded territory of the xʷməθkʷəy̓əm (Musqueam), Sḵwx̱wú7mesh (Squamish), and səlilwətaɬ (Tsleil-Waututh) peoples.

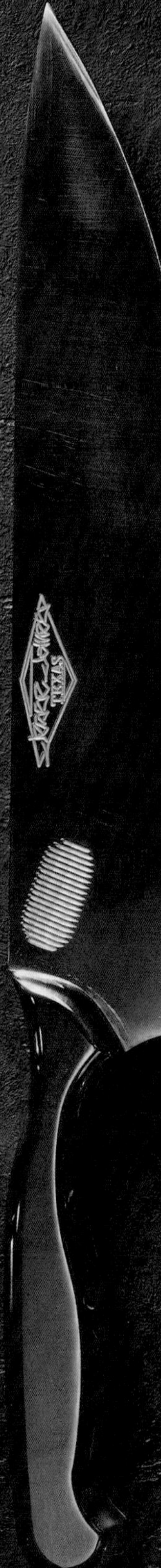

## RECIPE NOTES

**Unless stated otherwise:**

Butter is unsalted.
Eggs are large.
Herbs and citrus juices are fresh.
Black pepper is freshly ground.
Cheese is freshly grated or shredded.
Vegetables are medium-sized.
Worcestershire sauce is gluten-free.

# CONTENTS

THE KING OF

# BRUNCH

**I'VE ALWAYS DREAMED** of writing a cookbook to tell the story of my life as a restaurateur. And now, I get to share my crazy brunch addiction with all of you.

But let's start at the beginning, when I opened Hash Kitchen as a failing restaurateur. In 2013, I opened an upscale, bad-ass Italian seafood restaurant called Cuttlefish in Scottsdale, Arizona. Like most chefs, I created menus based on my palate and what I like to cook. Maybe Cuttlefish was before its time or we didn't execute the concept properly, but we struggled. My beautiful wife—Cristina—and I worked so hard to make it succeed, but it didn't make sense to go down with the ship. I had to change the concept and introduce people to another passion.

I thought to myself, You know what? We LOVE brunch. I'll flip this place into a fun brunch concept! My father and best friend, Tomaso Maggiore, the master chef and legendary restaurateur, told me, "You're crazy!

Do you know how many eggs you'll have to cook to make money?" Ha! My mom, Patricia, on the other hand, always encouraged me to open a breakfast concept, so our family had mixed emotions.

I'm vibrant, entertaining, and as wild as they get, so I decided to open something that reflected my personality. It was out of our comfort zone, but we did it, anyway. In 2015, we reopened as Hash Kitchen, serving brunch seven days a week. Cristina designed the décor, saying, "We have to make it like you: out-of-the-box and crazy, with a little Liberace style." (What can I say? I like things loud, shiny, and gold.) We transformed our oyster bar into a build-your-own Bloody Mary bar, created an unbelievable menu with nostalgic dishes and Instagram appeal, hired a DJ, and tagged the walls with #HashHashBaby! Hash Kitchen was so left field and different from what everyone else was doing at the time that it was immediately successful.

On opening weekend, there were only three of us in the kitchen, and Cristina had to help expedite the guests' orders. Who knew that there were so many ways to cook an egg? We were in the weeds. The first two weeks were rough, but we realized we had NAILED it once we got through them. We had created a destination restaurant where everyone wanted to go.

Cristina played an essential role when I was designing the menu as she has the sweet tooth in the family. Sure, I'm a sweet guy, but when I started creating the dishes, the menu was heavy on savory. With her help, we created an exciting menu that appealed to all palates.

We've got Bread Pudding French Toast Sticks (page 53), Blue Corn Bananas Foster Pancakes (page 62), and Crème Brûlée Waffles with Strawberries (page 77). I love translating dishes I was raised on into new and fun dishes, so it was time to introduce Cannoli Donuts to the world (page 39). We redefined the hash game with Carnitas Hash (page 109) and Gnocchi Carbonara Hash (page 121); we also added Fried Chicken (page 134) and potato skins (page 85) to our Benedicts.

I'm all about going bigger and better to maintain the fun vibe: the breakfast lasagna has ten layers (page 146); my Bao Buns are filled with birria (page 93); we've got sausage gravy poured onto Yorkshire puddings (page 150); and Billionaire's Bacon is glazed with yuzu and brown sugar and decorated with gold leaf (page 133).

And with amazing food, you need amazing drinks. I believe in drinking at any time of the day (in moderation, of course), so why not start at brunch? Bloody Marys pair well with savory foods, and mimosas enhance everything on the sweet side. Our mimosa flights and Mega Mimosa (topped with cotton candy) took off. For all the budding Bloody Mary stylists out there, we handed guests the mug, offered a choice of infused vodkas and house-made mixes, and encouraged them to go to town with over seventy toppings, from meatballs to every pickle imaginable.

There are also the Boozy Barista coffee cocktails (page 30) and disco ball drinks. Oh, and the cereal cocktails with my little twists on nostalgia because we love having fun. Remember eating cereal as a kid and the taste of that delicious leftover milk? Well, how about

drinking it spiked? We threw alcohol into ours and realized this grown-up version tasted even better.

But brunch isn't just about the food and bad-ass drinks. It's about the experience, and music is just as crucial in creating a vibe. A Chef Joey brunch is in your face, and we want to party seven days a week. That's why we've included Arizona's BEST deejay, DJ Ice, to design the set list (page 15) for your daytime brunch club.

When my three kids were younger, the all-important Sunday morning question would be, "What are you going to cook?" We always made brunch entertaining, and that's something I want to share with you. These recipes are fun, unique, and simple to execute—they are designed to be enjoyed with your family and friends in your home. Imagine waking up, having a wild brunch party, and then relaxing the rest of the day! Invite your friends over, turn up the volume,

and create some incredible memories with your own Chef Joey brunch with delicious food, the coolest cocktails, and amazing music courtesy of DJ Ice.

Hash, Hash, Baby!

## CHEF JOEY

---

### DIETARY SYMBOLS

- **VEG** Vegetarian
- **V** Vegan
- **GF** Gluten-free
- **DF** Dairy-free
- **NF** Nut-free

# SET THE *Vibe*

**MUSIC HAS ALWAYS BEEN** a love and a passion. I grew up cooking breakfast in the kitchen with my Nana, Papa, and Bama to the sound of '50s and '60s classics, including Smokey Robinson, Frank Sinatra, and The Beach Boys. At cookouts and family functions, music was a way to stimulate wonderful memories and create new ones. The dance party would kick off with '70s disco, '80s funk, and '90s cumbia; the drinks were always flowing.

I love to set moods the way Joey does with his menu, whether pairing the music with food and drinks at an establishment or cooking at home with the family. Each chapter of this book partners with a unique genre and musical flavors, and each playlist has its own personality. The track lists are designed to capture the ambiance of cooking along with Chef Joey in your kitchen. As the taste buds are being activated, the airwaves are being curated.

Readers can now experience some of the ambiance we have at the restaurants by re-creating Chef Joey's amazing food in their homes and joining us on this musical journey. Food and music make the world go round.

**DJ ICEMAN**
**@IMDJICEMAN**

## THE PLAYLISTS

**CHAPTER 1**
**MORNING REMIX**

**CHAPTER 2**
**FRENCH TOAST & MORE**

**CHAPTER 3**
**BAKED & GRIDDLED**

**CHAPTER 4**
**LET'S GET CRACKING**

**CHAPTER 5**
**HASH, HASH, BABY**

**CHAPTER 6**
**CHEF JOEY'S BRUNCH LIFE**

**CHAPTER 7**
**BACK TO BASICS**

# YOU BRING THE Hangover; I'LL BRING THE Cure.

# MORNING REMIX

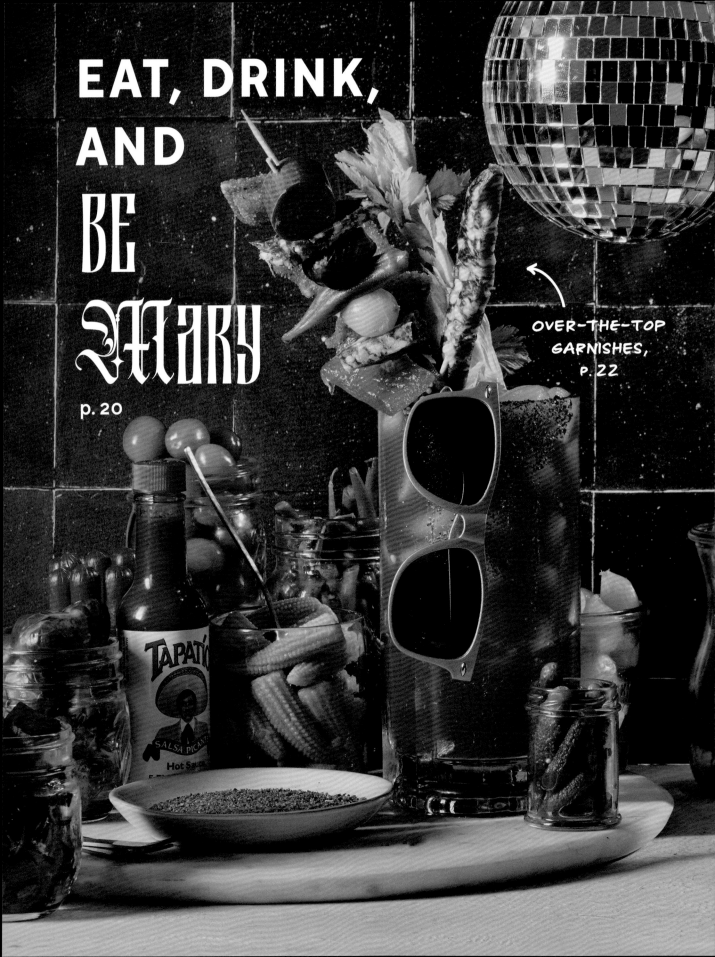

EAT, DRINK, AND BE *Mary*

p. 20

OVER-THE-TOP GARNISHES, P. 22

# EAT, DRINK *and* BE MARY

This iconic cocktail is known for its curative hangover effects, and after a night of over-indulgence, the only way to start the next day is with an amazing Bloody Mary that eases into brunch.

These three mixes will make your home the best Bloody Mary bar in town. And when it comes to embellishing your beverage, have some fun with it! At the restaurant, we garnish it to the extreme, and I encourage you to do the same.

## GREEN BLOODY MARY MIX

15 oz Salsa Verde (page 166)
4 fl oz Demitri's Classic Bloody
  Mary Seasoning
2 fl oz water
1 fl oz lime juice
1 fl oz lemon juice
1 tsp celery salt
1 tsp Worcestershire sauce
4 dashes Tabasco

## CHEF JOEY'S BLOODY MARY MIX

10 fl oz Demitri's Classic Bloody
  Mary Seasoning
5 oz Salsa Rojo (page 165)
5 fl oz tomato juice
2 fl oz water
1 fl oz lime juice
1 fl oz lemon juice
1 tsp celery salt
1 tsp Worcestershire sauce
4 dashes Tabasco

## TOO HOTT!!! BLOODY MARY MIX

10 oz Salsa Rojo (page 165)
10 fl oz Demitri's Chipotle-Habanero
  Bloody Mary Seasoning
2 fl oz hot sauce (preferably
  Valentina Salsa Picante)
1 fl oz lime juice
1 fl oz lemon juice
1 tsp celery salt
1 tsp Worcestershire sauce

# BLOODY MARY BAR

### 1. PICK YOUR RIM
- CELERY SALT
- BACON SALT

### 2. PICK YOUR VODKA
- CUCUMBER
- JALAPEÑO
- DIRTY VODKA
- CELERY
- CILANTRO LIME
- BACON

### 3. HOW SPICY?
- CLASSIC MIX 🌶
- TOMATILLO 🌶
- CHILI PEPPER 🌶🌶
- HABANERO 🌶🌶🌶🌶

### UPCHARGE +$4
- TITOS
- GREYGOOSE
- KETELONE
- PATRON SILVER
- JAMESON

## BIG #ASH
### BLOODY MARY 32oz
### $34

CALABRIAN CHILI

HORSERADISH

BABY GOT BRUNCH

# BUILD YOUR OWN
# Bloody Mary

Combine **1 part seasoning** and **1 part alcohol** with **5 parts mix** and **garnishes**. For example, **seasoning + 2 oz gin + 10 oz Green Bloody Mary Mix + Calabrian chiles = 1 helluva drink.**

## THE SEASONING (1 PART)

- 1 tsp Tajin
- 1 tsp lime juice

*Sprinkle Tajin over a shallow plate. Dip the top of a glass in lime juice and roll in Tajin to coat the rim.*

## THE VIBE (1 PART)

- Gin
- Tequila
- Vodka

## THE MIX (5 PARTS)

- Green Bloody Mary Mix
- Chef Joey's Bloody Mary Mix
- Too Hott!!! Bloody Mary Mix

## OVER-THE-TOP GARNISHES

*Set out a container of skewers, and let your guests create extravagant statements—the bigger, the better.*

| SOMETHING HEARTY | SOMETHING PIQUANT | SOMETHING SPICY | SOMETHING MEATY | SOMETHING ACIDIC |
|---|---|---|---|---|
| · Baby corn | · Blue cheese-stuffed olives | · Calabrian chiles | · Corndogs | · Lemon |
| · Brussels sprouts | · Pickled vegetables: asparagus, cauliflower, fennel, green beans, mushrooms, okra, red peppers, tomatillos, and zucchini | · Cherry peppers | · Cured chorizo | · Lime |
| · Celery | | · Horseradish | · Meatballs | |
| · Cocktail onions | | · Jalapeño poppers | · Salami | |
| · Garlic | | | | |
| · Hearts of palm | | | | |
| · Mozzarella | | | | |
| · Sun-dried tomatoes | | | | |
| · Tomatoes | | | | |

# ℭOMBINE

**1 PART SEASONING
AND 1 PART ALCOHOL
WITH 5 PARTS MIX
AND GARNISHES.**

# Mimosas

## MADE ME DO IT

p. 26

FRUIT JUICE
OR PURÉE
(1 PART)

THE BUBBLES
(4 PARTS)

# *Mimosas* MADE ME DO IT

While the classic mimosa combination of champagne or sparkling wine with orange juice is simple and elegant, encourage your guests to create their mimosa flights with different juices.

Start with your favorite sparkling wine—a budget-friendly option, such as Spanish cava or Italian prosecco, or something bougie, like French champagne.

Wait, there's more. Garnishes bring a mimosa to life. Crazy-looking pop rocks and cotton candy add not only sweetness and flavor but also nostalgic flair and wow factor. You can easily find most garnish items on Amazon, so let your imagination run wild. The sky's the limit, and playing with garnishes is a fun way to bring out your inner child.

---

The perfect ratio is **4:1 of bubbly** to **fruit juice** or **purée**. For example,

**8 fl oz prosecco + 2 fl oz blueberry purée = mimosa time.**

---

## THE BUBBLES (4 PARTS)

- Cava
- Champagne
- Flavored tonic
- Prosecco

**+**

## FRUIT JUICE OR PURÉE (1 PART)

- Blueberry
- Grapefruit
- Kiwi
- Mango
- Orange
- Peach
- Pineapple
- Strawberry

**+**

## GARNISHES

- Cotton candy
- Edible glitter
- Fruit boba (see Note)
- Pop rocks
- Sour candy

*Make simple syrup* by combining 1 cup granulated sugar and 1 cup water in a small saucepan. Bring to a boil and stir to combine until sugar has dissolved. Chill.

Blend 2 cups fresh fruit in a blender. Add 1 cup chilled simple syrup and blend again. Adjust taste to desired sweetness. Strain to remove any seeds. Chill before serving. Makes 3 cups.

Leftover purée can be stored in an airtight container in the fridge for 4–6 days.

**NOTE** Boba, or tapioca pearls, are small chewy balls made from tapioca starch that add visual appeal and texture to your favorite mimosa. Fruit boba are infused with fruit essences or juices, such as strawberry, mango, lychee, and passion fruit. Look for them at Asian markets, specialty tea shops, and online purveyors.

# THE
# PERFECT RATIO

## IS 4:1

## OF BUBBLY

## TO FRUIT JUICE

## OR PURÉE.

# Boozy Barista

p. 30

ITALIAN
ESPRESSO
MARTINI
P. 30

SALTED
CARAMEL
P. 30

# BOOZY BARISTA

Everyone loves coffee and alcohol, so why not combine them for something even more amazing? I like Monin syrups for flavoring because they're readily available and part of a well-established brand known for its high quality.

**Each recipe serves one, but you can scale up the recipe to suit your party.**

## SALTED CARAMEL

¼ cup granulated sugar
2 fl oz store-bought caramel drizzle
1 fl oz half-and-half
2 fl oz espresso
1½ fl oz vanilla vodka
1 fl oz salted caramel syrup (such as Monin)
1 fl oz cookie butter syrup (such as Monin)
Whipped Coffee Froth (page 31 [S'More])

Combine sugar and 1 tablespoon of water in a small saucepan and heat over medium heat. Allow the edges to brown and move the pan without stirring until the entire mixture is golden brown, about 10 minutes.

Line a baking tray with parchment paper and spoon thin strands of the sugar mixture over the parchment. Cool the strands for 3 minutes and using gloves spool the strands to form a nest. Cool for 5 minutes.

Drizzle caramel in a decorative pattern along the inside of a tall glass, reserving some for garnish. Fill the glass with ice. Pour in half-and-half.

In a cocktail shaker with ice, combine espresso, vodka, and syrups. Shake vigorously for 15 seconds.

Pour cocktail into the glass. Top with whipped coffee froth and garnish with more caramel drizzle. Top with sugar nest. Serve with a straw.

## ITALIAN ESPRESSO MARTINI

1 fl oz chilled espresso
1½ fl oz Amaro Averna
½ fl oz Kahlua
Shaved bittersweet (dark) chocolate (70% cocoa), for garnish

Combine all ingredients except chocolate in a cocktail shaker. Add ice, shake vigorously for 30 seconds, and strain into a chilled coupe glass. Garnish with shaved chocolate.

S'MORE
P. 31

TIRAMISU
P. 31

# S'MORE

## WHIPPED COFFEE FROTH
4 oz granulated sugar
1 oz instant coffee granules

## S'MORE
1 graham cracker, halved
1 chocolate bar, halved
2 large marshmallows

## ASSEMBLY
3 fl oz espresso
1½ fl oz whipped cream vodka
1 fl oz half-and-half
1 fl oz vanilla syrup (such as Monin)
1 fl oz dark chocolate syrup (such as Monin)
1 fl oz toasted marshmallow syrup (such as Monin)
Whipped Coffee Froth (see here)
1 oz Marshmallow Fluff, for garnish
S'More (see here)

**WHIPPED COFFEE FROTH** In a stand mixer fitted with the whisk attachment, mix all ingredients. Pour in 4 fl oz hot water and blend for 6–8 minutes on high speed, until light and frothy. (Alternatively, use a hand blender.)

**S'MORE** Thread half the graham cracker onto a skewer, followed by half the chocolate and both marshmallows. Thread the remaining chocolate and graham cracker. Using a torch, caramelize the marshmallows until slightly charred.

**ASSEMBLY** In a cocktail shaker with ice, combine all ingredients except whipped coffee froth, Marshmallow Fluff, and s'more and shake vigorously for 15 seconds.

Fill a tall glass with ice. Pour cocktail into the glass. Top with whipped coffee froth and garnish with Marshmallow Fluff. Place s'more on top. Serve with a straw.

# TIRAMISU

½ fl oz half-and-half
1½ fl oz vanilla vodka
3 fl oz espresso
1½ fl oz Mr. Black Cold Brew Coffee Liqueur
½ oz (1 tsp) mascarpone
1 fl oz vanilla syrup (such as Monin)
1 fl oz dark chocolate syrup (such as Monin)
1 fl oz tiramisu syrup (such as Monin)
Whipped Coffee Froth (page 31 [S'More])
2 ladyfingers, for garnish (see Note)

Fill a tall glass with ice. Pour in half-and-half.

In a cocktail shaker with ice, combine vodka, espresso, Mr. Black Cold Brew Coffee Liqueur, mascarpone, and all syrups. Shake vigorously for 15 seconds.

Pour cocktail into the glass. Top with whipped coffee froth and garnish with ladyfingers. Serve with a straw.

> **NOTE** A ladyfinger is an Italian egg-based cookie in the shape of, you guessed it, a finger. Ladyfingers can be purchased at finer grocery stores and Italian markets.

# Cereal Drinks

p. 34

COCOA
CRISPIES
P. 34

THE BEDROCK P. 35

# CEREAL DRINKS

I wanted to bring back that childhood memory of the deliciously flavored milk left in your cereal bowl—but in the form of a boozy drink. We serve them in the branded single-serve plastic cereal cups. These popular cups can be purchased in four- or six-packs at your local grocery store.

**Each recipe serves one, but you can scale up the recipe to suit your party.**

## COCOA CRISPIES

½ cup Cocoa Krispies cereal,
  plus extra for sprinkling
1½ fl oz vanilla vodka
1½ fl oz half-and-half
1 fl oz espresso
½ fl oz dark chocolate syrup
  (such as Monin)
½ fl oz vanilla syrup
2 oz whipped cream
4 oz Hershey's Chocolate Syrup

Put cereal in a blender or food processor and blend to a powder. Fill a Cocoa Krispies cereal cup to the top with ice.

In a cocktail shaker with ice, combine vodka, half-and-half, espresso, syrups, and Cocoa Krispies powder. Shake vigorously for 15 seconds.

Pour cocktail into the cup. Top with whipped cream and sprinkle with cereal. Drizzle with chocolate syrup. Serve with a straw.

# THE BEDROCK

**FRUITY PEBBLES TREATS**

½ cup (1 stick) butter,
  plus extra for greasing
1¼ cups mini marshmallows
  (divided)
5 cups Fruity Pebbles cereal

**THE BEDROCK**

5 Tbsp Fruity Pebbles cereal,
  plus extra for garnish
3 fl oz half-and-half
1½ fl oz vanilla vodka
1 fl oz blue curaçao
2 oz whipped cream
Fruity Pebbles Treats (see here),
  for garnish

**FRUITY PEBBLES TREATS**   Grease an 8-inch square baking dish with butter.

Melt butter in a large saucepan over low heat. Don't let the butter burn. Fold in ¾ cup marshmallows and stir gently until the marshmallows begin to melt. Remove pan from heat.

Stir in cereal and mix until well coated. Add the remaining ½ cup marshmallows and stir until melted and incorporated. With a buttered spatula, press the mixture into the prepared baking dish. Set aside to cool for 1 hour.

Using a cookie cutter, cut out fun shapes for cocktail garnishes. Any remaining Fruity Pebbles treats can be stored in an airtight container for 1 day.

**THE BEDROCK**   Put cereal in a mini blender or food processor and blend to a powder. Fill a Fruity Pebbles cereal cup to the top with ice.

In a cocktail shaker with ice, combine half-and-half, vodka, curaçao, and Fruity Pebbles powder. Shake vigorously for 15 seconds.

Pour cocktail into the cup. Top with whipped cream. Garnish with a Fruity Pebbles treat shape and a sprinkle of Fruity Pebbles cereal. Serve with a straw.

# Gangsta Sweets:

## SO GOOD

## IT'S ALMOST

## CRIMINAL.

# CHAPTER 2

# FRENCH TOAST & MORE

# CANNOLI DONUTS

As an Italian, I've always had cannoli in my life—and who doesn't love a donut? Here, I've combined two classic sweet treats by stuffing a donut with a sweetened ricotta cream. They're super sexy, absolutely money, and delicious straight out of the fryer.

**PART 1**

7 fl oz (213 g) whole milk
2 eggs (100 g), beaten
2½ Tbsp (31 g) granulated sugar
1½ Tbsp (14 g) instant dry yeast
2 Tbsp (43 g) honey
2 cups (255 g) all-purpose flour

**PART 2**

4 cups (510 g) all-purpose flour,
  plus extra for dusting
½ cup (96 g) shortening
2½ tsp (13 g) kosher salt

**ASSEMBLY**

4 cups canola oil
Donuts (see here)
2 cups Cannoli Cream (page 172)
Amarena cherries, for garnish
Confectioners' sugar, for dusting

**PART 1**  Place all ingredients in a medium bowl. Add 6½ fl oz (187 g) room-temperature water and mix thoroughly until smooth. Cover with plastic wrap and leave the bowl in a warm place for 1 hour, until the mixture has doubled in size.

**PART 2**  Place the dough mixture in the bowl of a stand mixer fitted with the hook attachment. Add all ingredients and mix for 8–10 minutes on the lowest speed, until the dough is cohesive. Cover and rest for 20 minutes.

Turn out on a lightly floured surface and roll the dough to a ½-inch thickness. Cut out 12 donut shapes, reserving donut holes. Arrange donut shapes and holes on a parchment-lined baking sheet, then cover with plastic wrap.

Donuts can be stored in the fridge for up to 2 days or frozen until needed.

**ASSEMBLY**  Heat oil in a deep 12-inch skillet over medium-high heat until it reaches a temperature of 350°F.

Working in batches to avoid overcrowding, carefully lower donuts and donut holes into the hot oil. Fry for 1½ minutes, until the bottom side is golden brown. Flip and fry for another 1½ minutes, until both sides are golden brown. Using a slotted spoon, transfer donuts to a paper towel–lined plate to drain excess oil. Repeat with the remaining donuts and donut holes.

To serve, place three donuts on each plate. Fill a piping bag with cannoli cream, then fill each donut center with cream. (Alternatively, fill a zip-top bag with cream, push out excess air, and reseal the bag. Snip a corner of the bag. Then, you're ready to pipe the cream.) Top each filled donut with a fried donut hole and garnish with cherries and a dusting of confectioners' sugar.

# *That* FUNKY MONKEY BREAD

**SERVES 2–4**

**VEG**

This delicious, pull-apart bread is perfect for sharing as an appetizer. It's a dish you can set out for your guests while you prepare the rest of the meal.

**CINNAMON SUGAR**
1 cup granulated sugar
2 tsp ground cinnamon

**BROWN-SUGAR GLAZE**
½ cup Cinnamon Sugar (see here)
½ cup packed brown sugar
1 cup (2 sticks) butter

**ASSEMBLY**
Cooking spray
½ cup Cinnamon Sugar (see here)
¼ cup chopped walnuts,
  plus extra for garnish
32 oz (907 g) store-bought or
  homemade Buttermilk Biscuit
  dough (page 175)
Brown-Sugar Glaze (divided,
  see here)

**CINNAMON SUGAR**  Mix all ingredients in a small bowl and set aside.

**BROWN-SUGAR GLAZE**  Combine all ingredients in a small saucepan over medium heat. Bring to a boil to dissolve sugar, then immediately remove from heat.

**ASSEMBLY**  Preheat oven to 350°F. Spray an 8-inch cake or loaf pan with cooking spray.

Place cinnamon sugar and walnuts in a zip-top bag. Cut the dough into bite-size pieces and place in the bag. Shake until dough pieces are fully coated. Place coated pieces in the pan and top with half the brown-sugar glaze. Bake for 30 minutes.

Use kitchen tongs to invert the monkey bread onto a plate. Garnish with walnuts, drizzle with the remaining brown-sugar glaze, and serve. Be careful—it's hot!

# CRÈME BRÛLÉE BRUSCHETTA

**SERVES 4**

Bruschetta is a staple in our Italian household. So naturally, I had to transform it into a decadent Italian breakfast! My bruschetta takes the excitement up a notch by topping buttery brioche with creamy crème brûlée, crispy sugar, and sweet strawberries.

1 Tbsp butter
6 slices brioche bread, each cut into 3- by 1- by 1-inch batons
1½ cups Crème Brûlée Custard (page 174)
3 Tbsp brown sugar
12 strawberries, sliced
Confectioners' sugar, for dusting
Sprigs of mint, for garnish

Preheat broiler over high heat.

Melt butter in a hot griddle or large nonstick pan over medium heat. Add bread and toast for 2 minutes on each side, until golden brown. Transfer to a baking sheet.

Top each baton with a layer of crème brûlée custard, then sprinkle with brown sugar. Broil for 2–3 minutes, until sugar is caramelized. (Or get the kitchen torch out and treat your guests to a show.) Arrange strawberries over caramelized sugar and dust with confectioners' sugar. Garnish with mint.

# Classic
# FRENCH TOAST

**SERVES 2**

**VEG** **NF**

I ask myself why anyone would want to mess with good bread (ha!), but my wife, Cristina, loves French toast—and she's not the only one. Enriched with eggs, challah and brioche are the best breads for French toast because they soak up the custard batter without getting too soggy and still maintain their structure.

## FRENCH TOAST BATTER
⅓ cup whole milk
1 tsp vanilla extract
4 eggs, beaten
2 Tbsp granulated sugar
1 tsp ground cinnamon
⅓ tsp ground nutmeg

## ASSEMBLY
2 Tbsp butter
4 slices brioche or challah bread, about 2 inches thick
2 cups French Toast Batter (see here)
½ cup maple syrup
1 Tbsp confectioners' sugar

**FRENCH TOAST BATTER**  In a large shallow bowl, whisk milk, vanilla, and eggs until combined.

In a small bowl, combine sugar, cinnamon, and nutmeg. Whisk into the egg mixture until combined.

The batter can be stored in an airtight container in the fridge for up to 2 days.

**ASSEMBLY**  Melt butter in a large nonstick pan or griddle over medium-high heat.

Dip bread slices into the batter, coating both sides and allowing excess to drip off. Add them to the pan, then cook for 2–3 minutes, until golden brown. Flip and repeat.

To serve, place two slices of French toast on each plate. Drizzle with maple syrup and dust with confectioners' sugar.

*Banana Split* **FRENCH TOAST** p. 48

# *Banana Split*
# FRENCH TOAST

**SERVES 2**

**VEG** **NF**

This bad-ass French toast has caramelized bananas and sweet mascarpone. I've added an Italian element with the mascarpone cone on top for the wow factor. It's delicious and decadent, but you can eat the whole thing without going into a sugar coma.

**SWEET MASCARPONE**
½ cup mascarpone
2¾ Tbsp confectioners' sugar
¼ tsp vanilla extract

**FRENCH TOAST BATTER**
⅓ cup whole milk
1 tsp vanilla extract
4 eggs, beaten
2 Tbsp granulated sugar
1 tsp ground cinnamon
⅓ tsp ground nutmeg

**SWEET MASCARPONE**  In a small bowl, combine all ingredients and whisk until well mixed.

**FRENCH TOAST BATTER**  In a large shallow bowl, whisk milk, vanilla, and eggs until combined.

In a small bowl, combine sugar, cinnamon, and nutmeg. Whisk into the egg mixture until combined.

The batter can be stored in an airtight container in the fridge for up to 2 days.

ASSEMBLY

2 Tbsp butter

4 slices brioche or challah bread,
  about 2 inches thick

2 cups French Toast Batter
  (see here)

¼ cup granulated sugar

2 bananas, halved lengthwise

½ cup Sweet Mascarpone
  (divided, see here)

2 small ice cream sugar cones

2 sprigs mint, for garnish

½ cup blueberries (divided),
  for garnish

4 strawberries, halved, for garnish

¾ cup maple syrup

2 Tbsp store-bought caramel
  sauce, warmed

1 Tbsp confectioners' sugar

**ASSEMBLY**  Melt butter in a large nonstick pan or griddle over medium-high heat.

Dip bread slices into the batter, coating both sides and allowing excess to drip off. Add them to the pan, then cook for 2–3 minutes until golden brown. Flip and repeat.

Sprinkle granulated sugar over bananas. Using a kitchen torch, caramelize until golden. (Alternatively, broil in the oven until sugar begins to brown.)

To serve, place a slice of French toast on a plate. Top with a layer of mascarpone, then layer with another piece of toast and 2 banana slices. Pipe or spoon mascarpone into a sugar cone, insert cone upright into the French toast stack, and garnish cone with mint and some blueberries.

Pipe or spoon more mascarpone onto the French toast. Garnish French toast with strawberries and the remaining blueberries, drizzle with maple syrup and caramel, and dust with confectioners' sugar. Repeat for the second serving.

# S'MORES FRENCH TOAST

**SERVES 2**

With graham crackers, marshmallows, and chocolatey Italian Nutella, this nostalgic dish brings back memories of great vacations, camping, or time spent with the family.

## NUTELLA ANGLAISE

1 cup whole milk
1 cup heavy cream
½ cup granulated sugar
8 medium egg yolks
⅓ cup Nutella

## FRENCH TOAST BATTER

⅓ cup whole milk
1 tsp vanilla extract
4 eggs, beaten
2 Tbsp granulated sugar
1 tsp ground cinnamon
⅓ tsp ground nutmeg

## ASSEMBLY

¼ cup (½ stick) butter
4 slices brioche or challah bread, about 2 inches thick
2 cups French Toast Batter (see here)
2 cups Nutella Anglaise (see here)
½ cup large marshmallows
Graham crackers

**NUTELLA ANGLAISE** Combine milk and cream in a small saucepan. Bring to a simmer over medium-high heat.

In a medium bowl, mix sugar and egg yolks until sugar is dissolved. Ladle a small amount of the milk mixture into the egg mixture, whisking continuously. (This tempers the eggs. If hot cream is added all at once, the eggs will scramble.) Keep adding ladles of the milk mixture, whisking continuously until custard is smooth.

Return the mixture to the saucepan and reduce heat to low. Cook, stirring frequently, until the mixture thickens enough to coat the back of a spoon. Strain the mixture to remove any bits of cooked egg. Fold in Nutella until thoroughly combined. Set aside to cool and store in the fridge until needed.

**FRENCH TOAST BATTER** In a large shallow bowl, whisk milk, vanilla, and eggs until combined.

In a small bowl, combine sugar, cinnamon, and nutmeg. Whisk into the egg mixture until combined.

The batter can be stored in an airtight container in the fridge for up to 2 days.

**ASSEMBLY** Melt butter in a large nonstick pan or griddle over medium-high heat.

Dip bread slices into the batter, coating both sides and allowing excess to drip off. Add them to the pan, then cook for 2–3 minutes, until golden brown. Flip and repeat.

To serve, place 1 slice of French toast on each plate. Spread ¼ cup Nutella anglaise over the slice. Add a layer of marshmallows. Top with a second slice and more Nutella anglaise. Finish with more marshmallows and graham crackers. For that s'mores look, use a kitchen torch to toast the marshmallows.

# Bread Pudding
# FRENCH TOAST STICKS

When my son was younger, he'd make us stop at McDonald's to get those fried French toast sticks on the way to school. I would tease him, telling him I could make them even **BETTER**. And that's what I did—in a traditional baked dessert with crème brûlée. He loved it.

**BREAD PUDDING STICKS**

8 slices brioche or challah bread, about 2 inches thick
2 Tbsp butter, melted
4 eggs, beaten
2 cups whole milk
½ cup granulated sugar
1 tsp vanilla extract
1 tsp ground cinnamon

**FRENCH TOAST BATTER**

⅓ cup whole milk
1 tsp vanilla extract
4 eggs, beaten
2 Tbsp granulated sugar
1 tsp ground cinnamon
⅓ tsp ground nutmeg

**BREAD PUDDING STICKS**  Preheat oven to 350°F. Line a 12- by 10-inch baking dish with parchment paper.

Cut bread into 1-inch cubes and spread out in a single layer across the prepared baking dish. Drizzle butter over bread and mix to evenly coat.

In a medium bowl, combine eggs, milk, sugar, vanilla, and cinnamon and whisk until mixed. Pour over bread and gently press down to ensure bread is soaked well with the milk mixture. Bake for 45 minutes, until the center is set. Set aside for 30 minutes to cool.

Place a layer of plastic wrap on top, then top with a similarly sized baking pan weighted with something heavy to compress bread pudding with even pressure. Refrigerate for at least 4 hours.

Remove bread pudding from the pan and transfer to a cutting board. Cut pudding into twelve ½- by ½- by 3-inch sticks.

Leftover French toast sticks can be stored in an airtight container in the fridge for up to 5 days or frozen for up to 3 months.

**FRENCH TOAST BATTER**  In a large shallow bowl, whisk milk, vanilla, and eggs until combined.

In a small bowl, combine sugar, cinnamon, and nutmeg. Whisk into the egg mixture until combined.

The batter can be stored in an airtight container in the fridge for up to 2 days.

*continued*

## ASSEMBLY

4 cups canola oil

12 Bread Pudding Sticks
  (see here)

2 cups French Toast Batter
  (see here)

¼ cup granulated sugar

1 tsp ground cinnamon

1 cup Crème Brûlée Custard
  (page 174)

Strawberries, sliced

Sprigs of mint, for garnish

Edible gold leaf flakes (optional),
  for garnish (see Note)

**ASSEMBLY**  Heat oil in a deep, large skillet over medium heat until it reaches a temperature of 350°F.

Coat bread pudding sticks in the batter, allowing excess to drip off. Working in batches to avoid overcrowding, carefully place sticks in the hot oil and deep-fry for 2 minutes, until golden brown. Using a slotted spoon, transfer French toast sticks to a paper towel–lined plate to drain excess oil. Repeat with the remaining sticks.

In a small bowl, combine sugar and cinnamon and mix well. Add French toast sticks and toss to coat.

Place four French toast sticks on a plate and add a layer of custard between each stick. Continue stacking French toast sticks until the dish is three layers high, adding custard between each stick.

Using a torch, gently caramelize French toast sticks and custard for that true brûlée feel. Place strawberries on the top layers. Garnish with mint and, if you want to bring it up to Chef Joey's level, some gold leaf flakes.

> **NOTE**  Edible gold leaf can be purchased in sheets or flakes, though flakes are easier to handle. Look for jars of flakes at cake and candy decorating shops and on Amazon.

# HOW YOU DOING,

## *Hot Cakes?*

# CHAPTER 3

# BAKED & GRIDDLED

# Better-than-Your-Mama's
# MALTED BUTTERMILK PANCAKES

**SERVES 2**

VEG  NF

My mom, Patricia, has always loved malts. She would tell us stories of going to the malt shop back in New York, so growing up, we loved them, too. When I opened my first burger concept, of course I had malts, and they went like crazy. Adding malted milk to pancakes and waffles gives them such a wonderful flavor.

**MALTED BUTTERMILK PANCAKE BATTER**

2 cups all-purpose flour
2 Tbsp malt powder
½ cup granulated sugar
1½ tsp baking powder
1½ tsp baking soda
1¼ tsp kosher salt
½ tsp ground cinnamon
2½ cups buttermilk
3 Tbsp butter, melted
1 Tbsp vanilla extract
2 eggs

**SALTED HONEY BUTTER**

¼ cup (½ stick) butter, room temperature
1 Tbsp honey
1 tsp kosher salt

**ASSEMBLY**

½ cup (1 stick) butter (divided)
4 cups Malted Buttermilk Pancake Batter (see here)
Salted Honey Butter (see here)
½ cup maple syrup

**MALTED BUTTERMILK PANCAKE BATTER** In a medium bowl, whisk flour, malt powder, sugar, baking powder, baking soda, salt, and cinnamon.

In a small bowl, whisk buttermilk, butter, vanilla, and eggs. Add wet ingredients to dry and whisk until smooth.

The batter can be stored in the fridge for up to 2 days.

**SALTED HONEY BUTTER** Combine all ingredients in a small bowl and mix well.

**ASSEMBLY** Heat a large nonstick pan or griddle over medium-high heat. Add 1 tablespoon of butter and tilt to coat the pan.

Pour in ½ cup batter and cook for 1½ minutes, until bubbles form along the edges and the underside is golden brown. Flip and cook for 1½ minutes, until golden brown. Transfer to a plate and cover with a dish towel to keep warm. Repeat with the remaining batter, adding more butter to the pan if necessary.

To serve, spread each pancake with salted honey butter and stack 4 per serving. Drizzle with maple syrup.

# CANNOLI PANCAKES

These pancakes are popular, especially with people who have a little Italian love in their souls. What's more nostalgic than a cannoli? Here, it's been reinvented as pancakes layered with cannoli cream and topped with Italian Amarena cherries bottled in syrup.

½ cup (1 stick) butter (divided)

½ tsp ground cinnamon

4 cups Malted Buttermilk Pancake Batter (page 59 [Better-than-Your-Mama's Malted Buttermilk Pancakes])

4 small cannoli shells (see Note)

2½ cups Cannoli Cream (divided, page 172)

8 Amarena cherries

Maple syrup

Confectioners' sugar

4 sprigs mint, for garnish

Chocolate chips, for garnish

Edible gold leaf flakes, for garnish (see Note)

Heat a large nonstick pan or griddle over medium-high heat. Add 1 tablespoon of butter and tilt to coat the pan.

Stir cinnamon into the batter. Pour in ½ cup batter and cook for 1½ minutes, until bubbles form along the edges and the underside is golden brown. Flip and cook for 1½ minutes, until golden brown. Transfer to a plate and cover with a dish towel to keep warm. Repeat with the remaining batter, adding more butter to the pan if necessary.

Using a piping bag, fill cannoli shells with some of the cannoli cream. (Alternatively, fill a zip-top bag with cream, push out excess air, and reseal the bag. Snip a corner of the bag. Then, you're ready to pipe the cream.)

Place a pancake on a plate. Spread ¼ cup of the remaining cannoli cream on top. Repeat with three more layers so you have a stack of four pancakes. Repeat on a second plate.

To serve, top each stack with 2 cannolis and 4 Amarena cherries. Drizzle with maple syrup and dust with confectioners' sugar. Garnish with 2 sprigs mint, chocolate chips, and gold leaf flakes.

> **NOTES** Cannoli shells are available at Italian markets or bakeries.
>
> Edible gold leaf can be purchased in sheets or flakes, though flakes are easier to handle. Look for jars of flakes at cake and candy decorating shops and on Amazon.

# Blue Corn
# BANANAS FOSTER PANCAKES

During a family vacation in Portland, we visited a restaurant with blue corn pancakes on the menu. What the hell are blue corn pancakes? I had to order them.

While I liked the flavor and the consistency, I knew we could do it better. So this is our version. The components combine with the caramelized bananas to create something unique, pretty, and tasty.

## BLUE CORN PANCAKE BATTER

¾ cup blue cornmeal (see Note)

1 tsp kosher salt

1 Tbsp agave nectar

½ cup whole milk, plus extra
  if needed

2 Tbsp butter, melted

1 egg, beaten

¾ cup all-purpose flour

2 tsp baking powder

## BANANAS FOSTER PANCAKES

¼ cup (½ stick) butter (divided)

2 cups Blue Corn Pancake Batter
  (see here)

1 banana

1 Tbsp granulated sugar

½ cup whipped cream

½ cup maple syrup

Ground cinnamon, for sprinkling

2 sprigs mint, for garnish

Chopped walnuts, for garnish

Confectioners' sugar, for garnish

**BLUE CORN PANCAKE BATTER** In a medium bowl, combine blue cornmeal and salt. Stir in agave nectar and 1 cup boiling water. Cover, then set aside to rest for 5 minutes.

Add milk, butter, and egg to the bowl and mix well. Fold in flour and baking powder until just incorporated. Do not overmix. The batter should coat a spoon but still run off smoothly. If the batter seems too thick, add more milk to thin it out.

The batter can be stored in the fridge for up to 2 days.

**BANANAS FOSTER PANCAKES** Heat a large nonstick pan or griddle over medium-high heat. Add 1 tablespoon of butter and tilt to coat the pan.

Pour in ½ cup batter. Cook for 1½ minutes, until bubbles form along the edges and the underside is golden brown. Flip and cook for 1½ minutes, until golden brown. Transfer to a plate and cover with a dish towel to keep warm. Repeat with the remaining batter, adding more butter to the pan if necessary.

Meanwhile, cut banana into large chunks. Sprinkle granulated sugar over each piece. Using a kitchen torch, caramelize until golden. (Alternatively, broil in the oven until sugar begins to brown.)

To serve, divide pancakes between two plates. Top with caramelized banana and whipped cream. Drizzle with maple syrup, sprinkle with cinnamon, and garnish with mint, walnuts, and confectioners' sugar.

> **NOTE** Blue cornmeal is made from ground blue corn. It has a slightly sweeter and nuttier flavor than white or yellow corn and is lower in starch. Adding boiling water helps to soften the cornmeal in the batter and give it a smoother texture.

# CARROT CAKE PANCAKES
## *with* CREAM CHEESE ICING

**SERVES 2**
**VEG** **NF**

This is a favorite of my corporate chef, Pierce Azlin. I'll let him share his story: "When I was growing up, my mom was always making carrot cake because it was one of my dad's favorites. Now, one of the best things about being a chef is the ability to recreate those tastes and memories while sharing something new. By combining a familiar breakfast dish like pancakes with this classic dessert, hopefully I'm able to bring back a memory for someone else."

### CARROT CAKE PANCAKE BATTER

2 cups all-purpose flour
½ cup granulated sugar
1¾ tsp baking powder
1 tsp ground cinnamon
¾ tsp ground nutmeg
¾ tsp baking soda
½ tsp kosher salt
¾ cup buttermilk
¾ cup whole milk
3 Tbsp + ½ tsp butter, melted
3 eggs, beaten
¾ cup grated carrots

### CREAM CHEESE ICING

¼ cup (½ stick) butter, softened
4 oz (½ cup) cream cheese, softened
½ tsp vanilla extract
Pinch of salt
2 cups confectioners' sugar

### ASSEMBLY

¼ cup (½ stick) butter
2 cups Carrot Cake Pancake Batter
  (see here)
1 baby carrot
1 Tbsp granulated sugar
¼ cup Cream Cheese Icing
  (see here)
Maple syrup
Confectioners' sugar, for dusting
Ground cinnamon, for sprinkling

**CARROT CAKE PANCAKE BATTER**  Sift flour, sugar, baking powder, cinnamon, nutmeg, baking soda, and salt into a large bowl. Whisk to combine.

In a medium bowl, whisk buttermilk, milk, butter, and eggs until smooth. Squeeze any moisture out of the carrots. Fold carrots into the batter. Add wet ingredients to dry and whisk until just combined. Do not overmix.

The batter can be stored in the fridge for up to 2 days.

**CREAM CHEESE ICING**  In the bowl of a stand mixer fitted with the whisk attachment, combine butter and cream cheese and beat until smooth and creamy. Add vanilla and salt and beat to incorporate. On the lowest speed, beat in confectioners' sugar until fully incorporated and smooth.

Refrigerate until needed. Leftover icing can be stored in an airtight container in the fridge for up to 3 days.

**ASSEMBLY**  Heat a large nonstick pan or griddle over medium-high heat. Add 1 tablespoon of butter and tilt the pan to coat.

Pour in ½ cup batter and cook for 1½ minutes, until bubbles form along the edges and the underside is golden brown. Flip and cook for 1½ minutes, until golden brown. Transfer to a plate and cover with a dish towel to keep warm. Repeat with the remaining batter, adding more butter to the pan if necessary.

Slice carrot in half. Sprinkle granulated sugar over cut side of carrot. Using a kitchen torch, gently caramelize until sugar is golden brown.

To serve, place a pancake on a plate. Slather cream cheese icing on top. Repeat with two more layers so you have a stack of three pancakes. Drizzle with maple syrup. Dust with confectioners' sugar and sprinkle with cinnamon. Dollop icing on top and place half the carrot on one side. Repeat for the second serving.

**GANGSTA SOUFFLÉ PANCAKES**
*with* **BERRY COMPOTE** p. 68

# GANGSTA SOUFFLÉ PANCAKES
## *with* BERRY COMPOTE

SERVES 2

VEG  NF

Soufflé pancakes are known for their light and airy texture, thanks to the incorporation of whipped egg whites into the batter. Soft and fluffy, they'll melt in your mouth.

**SOUFFLÉ PANCAKES**

6 eggs, separated
¼ cup milk
1 tsp vanilla extract
½ cup all-purpose flour
1 tsp baking powder
5 Tbsp granulated sugar
Cooking spray

**BERRY COMPOTE**

¾ cup granulated sugar
2 tsp vanilla extract
¼ tsp kosher salt
Grated zest and juice of 1 lemon
1 cup strawberries, halved
½ cup blueberries
½ cup blackberries
1 Tbsp cornstarch

**ASSEMBLY**

Soufflé Pancakes (see here)
1 cup Berry Compote (see here)
1 Tbsp confectioners' sugar
Cream Cheese Icing (page 64
  [Carrot Cake Pancakes with
  Cream Cheese Icing])
1 Tbsp confectioners' sugar
6 Tbsp maple syrup

**SOUFFLÉ PANCAKES**  Preheat oven to 350°F.

In a medium bowl, combine egg yolks, milk, and vanilla. Whisk until thick and frothy.

Sift flour and baking powder into a small bowl. Add to the milk mixture and mix until fully combined.

In a medium bowl or stand mixer fitted with the whisk attachment, combine sugar and egg whites and whisk until stiff peaks form. Using a spatula, gently fold meringue into the milk mixture until incorporated. Do not overmix.

Spray 2 small ovenproof skillets or 10-inch cake pans with cooking spray. Divide the batter between the pans. Bake for 10 minutes.

**BERRY COMPOTE**  In a small saucepan, combine sugar, vanilla, salt, and lemon zest and juice. Simmer over medium heat for 2 minutes. Add berries and cook for 3 minutes, until berries are softened.

In a small bowl, combine cornstarch and 2 tablespoons of water and mix well. (This is called a "slurry.") Pour into the saucepan and boil for 1 minute. Remove from heat. Makes 2 cups.

Leftover compote can be cooled, then stored in an airtight container in the fridge for up to 1 week.

**ASSEMBLY**  Arrange pancakes on two plates. Divide berry compote between each pancake. Dollop cream cheese icing on top. Dust with confectioners' sugar and drizzle with maple syrup.

# CINNAMON ROLL PANCAKES
## *with* CREAM CHEESE ICING

**SERVES 2**

**VEG**

My wife loves cinnamon rolls—and what's better than cinnamon sugar pancakes layered with cream cheese icing? They always make the kitchen smell great.

**CINNAMON ROLL PANCAKE BATTER**

2 cups all-purpose flour

½ cup granulated sugar

1 Tbsp ground cinnamon

1¾ tsp baking powder

¾ tsp baking soda

½ tsp kosher salt

1½ cups whole milk

3 Tbsp + ½ tsp butter, melted

3 eggs, beaten

**CREAM CHEESE ICING**

¼ cup (½ stick) butter, softened

4 oz (½ cup) cream cheese, softened

½ tsp vanilla extract

Pinch of salt

2 cups confectioners' sugar

**ASSEMBLY**

¼ cup (½ stick) butter

2 cups Cinnamon Roll Pancake Batter (see here)

¼ cup + 2 Tbsp Cream Cheese Icing (divided, see here)

2 store-bought cinnamon buns, cut into a smaller ring, for garnish

Chopped walnuts, for garnish

Maple syrup

**CINNAMON ROLL PANCAKE BATTER** Sift flour, sugar, cinnamon, baking powder, baking soda, and salt into a large bowl. Whisk to combine.

In a medium bowl, combine milk, butter, and eggs and whisk until smooth. Add wet ingredients to dry and whisk until just combined. Do not overmix.

The batter can be stored in the fridge for up to 2 days.

**CREAM CHEESE ICING** In a stand mixer fitted with the whisk attachment, combine butter and cream cheese and beat until smooth and creamy. Add vanilla and salt and beat to incorporate. On the lowest speed, beat in confectioners' sugar until fully incorporated and smooth.

Refrigerate until needed. Leftover icing can be stored in an airtight container in the fridge for up to 3 days.

**ASSEMBLY** Heat a large nonstick pan or griddle over medium-high heat. Add 1 tablespoon of butter and tilt the pan to coat.

Pour in ½ cup batter and cook for 1½ minutes, until bubbles form along the edges and the underside is golden brown. Flip and cook for another 1½ minutes, until golden brown. Transfer to a plate and cover with a dish towel to keep warm. Repeat with the remaining batter, adding more butter to the pan as necessary.

To serve, divide pancakes between two plates. Spread cream cheese icing on each pancake as you stack. Drizzle more icing over top. Garnish with a cinnamon bun and walnuts. Drizzle with maple syrup.

# BLING BLING BLINTZES

My daughter Giuliana would always order blintzes at restaurants, and I never liked the cottage cheese filling. This is a recipe for blintzes the way I would like to eat them—with ricotta and cream cheese to make them decadent.

And the cotton candy and the gold? What can I say? I'm a gold-decorated chef! I mean, have you seen my chains?

### FILLING
2 oz (¼ cup) cream cheese, softened
2½ Tbsp confectioners' sugar
1 cup cottage cheese
1 cup whole milk ricotta (such as Polly-O)
Grated zest of ½ lemon

### BLUEBERRY COMPOTE
¾ cup granulated sugar
2 tsp vanilla extract
¼ tsp kosher salt
Grated zest and juice of 1 lemon
2 cups blueberries
1 Tbsp cornstarch

### BLINTZES
¾ cup whole milk
½ cup all-purpose flour
2 Tbsp granulated sugar
¼ tsp kosher salt
½ tsp vanilla extract
1½ Tbsp butter, softened

### ASSEMBLY
Filling (see here)
Blintzes (see here)
2 Tbsp butter
Blueberry Compote (see here)
Confectioners' sugar, for dusting
½ cup strawberry cotton candy
1 tsp edible gold leaf flakes (see Note)

**FILLING**  In a medium bowl, combine cream cheese and confectioners' sugar and mix with a rubber spatula until smooth. Stir in cottage cheese, ricotta, and lemon zest and mix to combine.

Refrigerate until needed.

**BLUEBERRY COMPOTE**  In a small saucepan, combine sugar, vanilla, salt, and lemon zest and juice. Simmer over medium heat for 2 minutes. Add berries and cook for 3 minutes, until berries are softened.

In a small bowl, combine cornstarch and 2 tablespoons of water and mix well. (This is called a "slurry.") Pour into the saucepan and boil for 1 minute. Remove from heat. Makes 2 cups.

**BLINTZES**  Place all ingredients in a blender and blend until smooth.

Heat a medium skillet over medium heat. Pour in ¼ cup batter and swirl the skillet in a circular motion to form a thin disk. Cook for 2 minutes, until lightly golden. Flip and cook for another 2 minutes. Transfer to a plate and cover with a dish towel to keep warm. Repeat with the remaining batter.

**ASSEMBLY**  Spoon ¼ cup filling along the middle of each blintz. Carefully roll blintzes, tucking in both sides and the top to fully seal.

Melt butter in a large skillet over medium heat. Add filled blintzes and fry for 1 minute on each side, until golden brown.

To serve, transfer blintzes to a serving plate. Spoon blueberry compote over top and dust with confectioners' sugar. Decorate with tufts of cotton candy and gold leaf flakes.

> **NOTE**  Edible gold leaf can be purchased in sheets or flakes, though flakes are easier to handle. Look for jars of flakes at cake and candy decorating shops and on Amazon.

# DUTCH BABY
## *with* STRAWBERRY COMPOTE

**SERVES 2**
**VEG** **NF**

A Dutch baby, or German pancake, is baked in the oven until it puffs up and turns golden and crisp around the edges. At home, we usually have it with confectioners' sugar and whipped ricotta or mascarpone, but it can also be garnished with a fruit compote, as I've done here. Or for something savory, load it up with Birria (page 141) or Carnitas (page 139), fold it up, and you've made yourself a Dutch baby burrito!

### STRAWBERRY COMPOTE
¾ cup granulated sugar
2 tsp vanilla extract
¼ tsp kosher salt
Grated zest and juice of 1 lemon
2 cups strawberries, halved
1 Tbsp cornstarch

### DUTCH BABY BATTER
1 cup all-purpose flour
2 Tbsp granulated sugar
¼ tsp ground nutmeg
1 cup whole milk
6 eggs

### ASSEMBLY
½ cup (1 stick) butter (divided)
Dutch Baby Batter (see here)
1 cup Strawberry Compote
 (see here)
½ cup maple syrup
Confectioners' sugar, for dusting
1 lemon, halved, for garnish

**STRAWBERRY COMPOTE**  In a small saucepan, combine sugar, vanilla, salt, and lemon zest and juice. Simmer over medium heat for 2 minutes. Add strawberries and cook for another 3 minutes, until strawberries are softened.

In a small bowl, combine cornstarch and 2 tablespoons of water and mix well. (This is called a "slurry.") Pour into the saucepan and boil for 1 minute. Remove from heat.

Leftover compote can be cooled, then stored in an airtight container in the fridge for up to 1 week.

**DUTCH BABY BATTER**  Sift flour, sugar, and nutmeg into a medium bowl.

In a separate medium bowl, whisk milk and eggs. Add wet ingredients to dry and whisk until smooth.

The batter can be stored in the fridge for up to 1 day.

**ASSEMBLY**  Preheat oven to 425°F.

Divide butter between two 10-inch cast-iron pans. Place pans in the preheated oven for 2–3 minutes, until butter is melted but not colored. (If you don't have two pans, just make one Dutch baby at a time.)

Carefully pour half the batter into each pan, swirling to fill the pan to the edges. Bake for 20 minutes, until puffed and golden brown. (If making one Dutch baby at a time, refrigerate the remaining batter until needed.)

Reduce heat to 300°F. Bake for another 5 minutes, until completely cooked and a toothpick inserted into the center comes out clean. (Repeat with the remaining Dutch Baby.)

Place Dutch babies on two plates. Spoon strawberry compote into the center, drizzle with maple syrup, and dust with confectioners' sugar. Squeeze lemon juice over top and garnish with lemon.

# CRÈME BRÛLÉE WAFFLES
## *with* STRAWBERRIES

Level up your waffle game! Paired with fresh strawberries and velvety crème brûlée, with its crackly, caramelized sugar coating, these waffles transform comfort food into over-the-top indulgence.

**MALTED WAFFLE BATTER**

2 cups all-purpose flour

1 Tbsp granulated sugar

2 Tbsp malt powder

1 tsp kosher salt

1 tsp baking powder

1½ cups lukewarm whole milk

⅓ cup (⅔ stick) butter, melted

1 tsp vanilla extract

2 eggs, beaten

**CRÈME BRÛLÉE WAFFLES**

Cooking spray

4 cups Malted Waffle Batter
 (see here)

1 cup Crème Brûlée Custard
 (page 174)

1 Tbsp granulated sugar

6 strawberries, sliced

Confectioners' sugar, for dusting

Sprigs of mint, for garnish

Edible gold leaf flakes, for garnish
 (see Note)

**MALTED WAFFLE BATTER**  Sift flour, sugar, malt powder, salt, and baking powder into a large bowl. Whisk to combine.

In a medium bowl, combine milk, butter, vanilla, and eggs and whisk until well mixed. Add wet ingredients to dry and whisk until combined.

The batter can be stored in the fridge for up to 2 days or frozen for up to 1 month. If using frozen batter, thaw overnight in the fridge.

**CRÈME BRÛLÉE WAFFLES**  Preheat waffle iron according to the manufacturer's instructions.

Spray the waffle iron with cooking spray. Ladle half the batter onto the grill plate. Cook until golden brown. Place waffle on a plate. Repeat with the remaining batter.

Using a butter knife, spread crème brûlée custard over each waffle, making sure to fill in grid pockets. Sprinkle sugar over custard. Using a kitchen torch, torch sugar until golden brown and "burnt."

Decorate with strawberries and dust with confectioners' sugar. Garnish with mint and gold leaf flakes. Serve immediately.

> **NOTE** Edible gold leaf can be purchased in sheets or flakes, though flakes are easier to handle. Look for jars of flakes at cake and candy decorating shops and on Amazon.

# FRIED CHICKEN *and* WAFFLES

**SERVES 2**

**NF**

We lived in California when I was a teenager, and my first encounter with chicken and waffles was at Roscoe's, a popular soul food restaurant chain renowned for their chicken and waffles. I took my first bite and whoa! There was sweetness, saltiness, juicy chicken. I was like, What the heck is happening here? The delicious combination of crisp chicken, sweet waffles, and rich syrup brings back those memories.

### MALTED WAFFLE BATTER

2 cups all-purpose flour
1 Tbsp granulated sugar
2 Tbsp malt powder
1 tsp kosher salt
1 tsp baking powder
1½ cups lukewarm whole milk
⅓ cup (⅔ stick) butter, melted
1 tsp vanilla extract
2 eggs, beaten

### FRIED CHICKEN AND WAFFLES

Cooking spray
2 cups Malted Waffle Batter
  (see here)
Fried Chicken (page 134)
Fried Onions (page 109
  [Carnitas Hash])
Confectioners' sugar, for garnish
½ cup maple syrup

**MALTED WAFFLE BATTER** Sift flour, sugar, malt powder, salt, and baking powder into a large bowl. Whisk to combine.

In a medium bowl, combine milk, butter, vanilla, and eggs and whisk until well mixed. Add wet ingredients to dry and whisk until combined.

The batter can be stored in the fridge for up to 2 days or frozen for up to 1 month. If using frozen batter, thaw overnight in the fridge.

**FRIED CHICKEN AND WAFFLES** Preheat waffle iron according to the manufacturer's instructions.

Spray the waffle iron with cooking spray. Ladle half the batter onto the grill plate. Cook until golden brown. Place waffle on a plate. Repeat with the remaining batter.

To serve, top each waffle with fried chicken and fried onions. Garnish with confectioners' sugar and drizzle with maple syrup.

# THE CHEF IS COOKING;

# DON'T BREAK HIS EGGS.

# LET'S GET CRACKING

# POTATO SKIN BENEDICT

**SERVES 2**

**NF**

When I was a kid, my father always grumbled whenever I ordered potato skins. "What?!" he'd exclaim. "They give you the ends of the potato, and you eat that?" It was hilarious. Nostalgia definitely brought this dish to life.

## POTATO SKINS

2 russet potatoes, unpeeled
1 tsp olive oil
1 tsp kosher salt, plus extra
  to taste
2 Tbsp butter, melted
Black pepper, to taste
1 cup shredded sharp cheddar
½ cup chopped cooked bacon

## POTATO SKIN BENEDICT

1 Tbsp canola or olive oil
2 cups Brunch Potatoes
  (page 108)
4 eggs
2 Tbsp white vinegar
Potato Skins (see here)
8 strips cooked bacon
4 Tbsp sour cream
Kosher salt and black pepper
½ cup Chef Pierce Hollandaise
  (page 169)
2 cups Fried Onions (page 109
  [Carnitas Hash])
4 tsp sliced scallions,
  for garnish

**POTATO SKINS**  Preheat oven to 400°F. Line a baking sheet with aluminum foil.

Brush potatoes with oil and sprinkle with salt. Place on the prepared baking sheet and bake for 1 hour, until soft. Remove potatoes and set aside to cool. Increase oven temperature to 450°F.

When potatoes are cool enough to handle, halve them lengthwise. Using a spoon, scoop out flesh, leaving ¼ inch of the potato around the skin. (The scooped potatoes can be reserved for another use.)

Brush insides of potatoes with butter and season with salt and pepper. Bake for 10 minutes. Flip potato skins over and cook for another 5 minutes, until the edges become crispy.

Top with cheese and bacon and bake for another 3–5 minutes, until cheese is melted.

**POTATO SKIN BENEDICT**  Heat oil in a large cast-iron skillet over medium-high heat. Add potatoes and cook for 3 minutes, until hot. Keep warm.

Bring a medium saucepan of water to a boil.

Meanwhile, crack an egg into a fine-mesh sieve over a small bowl. Gently swirl the egg in the sieve so that the loose, watery egg white drains into the bowl. Place the intact egg in a separate small bowl. Repeat with the remaining eggs.

Stir vinegar into the boiling water, creating a vortex by vigorously stirring the water in a circle. Add an egg to the middle of the vortex and cook for 3 minutes. Using a slotted spoon, transfer egg to a paper towel–lined plate to drain excess water. Repeat with the remaining eggs.

Place two potato skins on each plate. Top with bacon and a drizzle of sour cream. Place eggs on top. Season eggs with salt and pepper. Pour hollandaise over eggs and top with fried onions. Garnish with scallions. Serve with brunch potatoes on the side.

# FRIED CHICKEN BENEDICT

SERVES 2

My go-to brunch meal is eggs Benedict. Poached is my favorite way to eat eggs, and I love the versatility of hollandaise. Take your time and don't screw up the eggs! It's a delicate dish, so don't get too excited and overboil it. Use a little vinegar and go slowly.

2 Tbsp butter
2 Buttermilk Biscuits (page 175), halved into disks
4 eggs
2 Tbsp white vinegar
Fried Chicken (page 134), halved
Kosher salt and black pepper
1 cup Chef Pierce Hollandaise (page 169)
2 Tbsp finely chopped chives, for garnish
1 cup Fried Onions (page 109 [Carnitas Hash]), for garnish
½ cup maple syrup

Melt butter in a skillet or griddle over medium-high heat. Add biscuits, cut side down. Cook for 2–3 minutes, until golden brown. Set aside.

Bring a medium saucepan of water to a boil.

Meanwhile, crack an egg into a fine-mesh sieve over a small bowl. Gently swirl the egg in the sieve so that the loose, watery egg white drains into the bowl. Place the intact egg in a separate small bowl. Repeat with the remaining eggs.

Stir vinegar into the boiling water, creating a vortex by vigorously stirring the water in a circle. Add an egg to the middle of the vortex and cook for 3 minutes. Using a slotted spoon, transfer egg to a paper towel–lined plate to drain excess water. Repeat with the remaining eggs.

Place two biscuit halves on each plate. Top with fried chicken, followed by eggs. Season eggs with salt and pepper. Pour ½ cup hollandaise over each, then garnish with chives and fried onions. Drizzle with maple syrup.

# Cristina's
# TAMALE CAKES BENEDICT

Back in the day, my wife, Cristina, made a delicious tamale cake that my kids loved, which inspired me to create this Benedict. It's been a big seller, but my wife deserves all the credit.

While both Maseca and cornmeal are made from dried corn, Maseca is a brand of fine masa flour while cornmeal is more coarsely ground. Using a combination of cornmeal and Maseca in this recipe, along with ground corn kernels, delivers more flavor and greater texture.

**TAMALE CAKES**

Cooking spray
4 cups frozen corn kernels
1 cup cornmeal
¾ cup granulated sugar
¼ cup corn masa flour
  (preferably Maseca)
½ cup (1 stick) butter, melted
¾ Tbsp baking powder

**TAMALE CAKES** Preheat oven to 225°F. Spray a baking sheet with cooking spray.

Place frozen corn kernels in a food processor and pulse until coarsely blended.

Transfer to a medium bowl, add the remaining ingredients, and mix well. Evenly spread the mixture onto the prepared baking sheet. Bake for 45 minutes, until a toothpick inserted into the center comes out clean.

Set aside to cool, then refrigerate for at least 4 hours. Cut into 2- x 4-inch rectangles.

Makes 6 cakes. Store in the fridge for up to 4 days or freeze for up to 3 months.

*continued*

## TAMALE CAKES BENEDICT

2 Tbsp canola or olive oil (divided)

2 cups Carnitas (page 139)

2 cups Brunch Potatoes (page 108)

4 eggs

2 Tbsp white vinegar

2 dried corn husks (see Note)

2 Tamale Cakes (see here),
  warmed

Kosher salt and black pepper

Fried Onions (page 109
  [Carnitas Hash])

½ cup Green Chile Hollandaise
  (page 170)

2 Tbsp finely chopped cilantro,
  for garnish

**TAMALE CAKES BENEDICT**  Heat 1 tablespoon of oil in a large cast-iron skillet over medium-high heat. Add carnitas and sauté for 3–4 minutes, until warmed through. Transfer to a medium bowl and cover with a dish towel to keep warm.

Heat the remaining tablespoon of oil in the same skillet over medium-high heat. Add potatoes and cook for 3 minutes, until hot. Keep warm.

Bring a medium saucepan of water to a boil.

Meanwhile, crack an egg into a fine-mesh sieve over a small bowl. Gently swirl the egg in the sieve so that the loose, watery egg white drains into the bowl. Place the intact egg in a separate small bowl. Repeat with the remaining eggs.

Stir vinegar into the boiling water, creating a vortex by vigorously stirring the water in a circle. Add an egg to the middle of the vortex and cook for 3 minutes. Using a slotted spoon, transfer egg to a paper towel–lined plate to drain excess water. Repeat with the remaining eggs.

To serve, arrange a corn husk on each plate and place a tamale cake on top. Top with carnitas and two eggs. Season eggs with salt and pepper. Top with fried onions. Finish with hollandaise and garnish with cilantro. Serve with potatoes on the side.

> **NOTE**  Dried corn husks are available in grocery stores and Mexican markets.

# BIRRIA BAO BENEDICT

SERVES 2

We're opening an Asian concept, so we've been toying around with new dishes. I love bao buns, so we had to do a brunch one! The baos are great with the eggs and birria. It looks sexy, but it's also super fun.

1 Tbsp olive or canola oil
1 cup Birria (page 141)
4 eggs
2 Tbsp white vinegar
4 Bao Buns (page 176)
1 cup Consommé (page 141)
Kosher salt and black pepper
½ cup Chef Pierce Hollandaise
  (page 169)
1 Tbsp chopped white onion
2 Tbsp chopped cilantro
1 lime, cut in quarters

Heat oil in a large skillet over medium-high heat. Add birria and sauté for 3–4 minutes, until warmed through. Transfer to a medium bowl and cover with a dish towel to keep warm.

Bring a medium saucepan of water to a boil.

Meanwhile, crack an egg into a fine-mesh sieve over a small bowl. Gently swirl the egg in the sieve so that the loose, watery egg white drains into the bowl. Place the intact egg in a separate small bowl. Repeat with the remaining eggs.

Stir vinegar into the boiling water, creating a vortex by vigorously stirring the water in a circle. Add an egg to the middle of the vortex and cook for 3 minutes. Using a slotted spoon, transfer egg to a paper towel–lined plate to drain excess water. Repeat with the remaining eggs.

Bring water to a boil in a wok or wide pan that fits a steamer or colander. Line the steamer with parchment paper. Steam buns for 1–2 minutes if refrigerated (or 3–4 minutes if frozen). Do not allow water to touch the buns.

Heat the same skillet over medium-high heat. Dip buns into consommé and place in the skillet. Cook for 1 minute on each side. Remove from heat.

Fill buns with birria. Place two buns on each plate and top with eggs. Season eggs with salt and pepper. Finish with hollandaise. Place onion, cilantro, lime, and consommé on the side.

**BIRRIA BAO BENEDICT** p. 93

# ZUCCHINI, POTATO, *and* ONION FRITTATA

Frittatas have always been a staple of our Italian household. They're easy to make and bring to gatherings. If you go to the beach or to a game, everybody brings frittatas. Since they're great at room temperature, they're perfect to snack on throughout the day, and this is the one we make the most often. I have fond memories of making my first frittata with my Uncle Arthur in New York, and this recipe has stayed with me my entire life.

12 eggs
Kosher salt and black pepper
2 Tbsp olive oil
1 small red onion, julienned
  (¼ cup)
1 zucchini, cut into ¼-inch-thick slices
4 slices provolone
2 Tbsp grated Parmesan,
  for garnish

Preheat oven to 400°F.

In a medium bowl, whisk eggs. Season with salt and pepper.

Heat oil in a large ovenproof skillet over medium-high heat. Add onion. Cook for 3 minutes, until onion has softened.

Pour the whisked eggs over the hot onion, arrange zucchini slices on top, then reduce heat to low. Cook for 2 minutes, until the eggs at the edges of the skillet begin to set. Make sure the edges do not burn. Remove from heat if needed.

Bake for 15–17 minutes, until eggs are fluffy and cooked through.

Top with provolone and bake for another minute, until cheese melts.

To serve, run a spatula around the edges of the skillet and slide the frittata onto a plate. Garnish with Parmesan and slice into wedges. Serve warm or at room temperature.

# Tomaso's
# SAUSAGE AND PEPPER FRITTATA

**SERVES 2**

GF   NF

My dad, Tomaso, made the best sausage known to mankind. For forty-six years at his eponymous Phoenix restaurant, Tomaso's, he made Sicilian sausage, and it's now one of those special family recipes. When I use it in a frittata, it brings back childhood memories. It's delicious in a sandwich, too.

12 eggs
Kosher salt and black pepper
2 Tbsp olive oil
1 cup cooked and sliced spicy
   Italian sausage
1 red bell pepper, seeded,
   deveined, and cut into strips
1 green bell pepper, seeded,
   deveined, and cut into strips
2 Tbsp grated Parmesan,
   for garnish
Sprig of oregano, for garnish

Preheat oven to 400°F.

In a medium bowl, whisk eggs. Season with salt and pepper.

Heat oil in a large ovenproof skillet over medium heat. Add sausage and peppers and sauté for 3 minutes, until warmed through.

Pour the whisked eggs over the hot ingredients, then reduce heat to low. Cook for 2 minutes, until the eggs at the edges of the skillet begin to set. Make sure the edges do not burn. Remove from heat if needed.

Bake for 15–17 minutes, until eggs are fluffy and cooked through.

To serve, run a spatula around the edges of the skillet and slide the frittata onto a plate. Garnish with Parmesan and oregano. Slice into wedges and serve warm or at room temperature.

Tomaso's
**SAUSAGE AND
PEPPER FRITTATA** p. 99

# TINGA FRITTATA

The chipotle adds a smoky flavor to the chicken tinga and makes this recipe shine. We wanted to make this frittata even more money, so we added black beans, corn, avocado, salsa verde, and sour cream. Every bite is packed with beautiful flavor.

12 eggs

Kosher salt and black pepper

½ cup fresh corn kernels

½ cup canned black beans, rinsed and drained

1 cup Chicken Tinga (page 143 [Chilaquiles])

2 tsp olive or canola oil

1 avocado, for garnish

½ cup Salsa Verde (page 166), for garnish

2 Tbsp sour cream, for garnish

2 Tbsp finely chopped cilantro, for garnish

2 Tbsp grated Cotija cheese, for garnish

Preheat oven to 400°F.

In a medium bowl, whisk eggs. Season with salt and pepper.

Heat a large ovenproof skillet over medium heat. Add corn and black beans and stir to combine. Cook for 2 minutes, until hot. Transfer to a small bowl and cover to keep warm.

In the same skillet over medium heat, heat chicken tinga until hot. Transfer to a bowl and cover to keep warm.

Heat oil in the same skillet over medium heat. Pour the whisked eggs into the skillet, then reduce heat to low. Cook for 2 minutes, until the eggs at the edges of the skillet begin to set. Make sure the edges do not burn. Remove from heat if needed.

Bake for 15–17 minutes, until eggs are fluffy and cooked through.

Meanwhile, halve avocado and remove pit. Thinly slice each half, fanning out the slices.

To serve, run a spatula around the edges of the skillet and slide the frittata onto a plate. Top with the corn mixture and chicken tinga. Garnish with salsa, sour cream, avocado, cilantro, and Cotija. Slice into wedges.

# SMOKED SALMON FRITTATA

**SERVES 2**

GF  NF

People love smoked salmon for breakfast, so we wanted to add that to the menu. This has all the traditional accompaniments, like tomatoes, capers, red onion, and dill, but is "hashified" as an amazing frittata.

12 eggs
Kosher salt and black pepper
2 Tbsp olive oil
½ cup cherry tomatoes, halved
1–2 Tbsp finely chopped chives
4 oz hot- or cold-smoked salmon
2 Tbsp mascarpone
1 Tbsp capers, for garnish
½ red onion, thinly sliced,
  for garnish
1 Tbsp chopped dill, for garnish

Preheat oven to 400°F.

In a medium bowl, whisk eggs. Season with salt and pepper.

Heat oil in a large ovenproof skillet over medium heat. Add tomatoes and chives and sauté for 2 minutes, until warmed through.

Pour the whisked eggs over the hot ingredients, then reduce heat to low. Cook for 2 minutes, until the eggs at the edges of the skillet begin to set. Make sure the edges do not burn. Remove from heat if needed.

Bake for 15–17 minutes, until eggs are fluffy and cooked through.

To serve, run a spatula around the edges of the skillet and slide the frittata onto a plate. Top with smoked salmon and mascarpone. Garnish with capers, onion, and dill. Slice into wedges.

# CHANGING THE BRUNCH GAME

## One Hash at a Time.

CHAPTER 5

# HASH, HASH, BABY

# BRUNCH POTATOES

MAKES ABOUT 4 CUPS

Stock these in your fridge for a staple to elevate your weekend brunches and breakfast sides.

**POTATO SEASONING**

1½ Tbsp granulated garlic

2 tsp kosher salt

1 tsp black pepper

1 tsp onion powder

¾ tsp paprika

½ tsp chopped rosemary

½ tsp chopped thyme

**BRUNCH POTATOES**

2 large russet potatoes
 (see Note)

1 Tbsp olive oil

1 white onion, chopped

1 large red bell pepper, seeded,
 deveined, and chopped

4 garlic cloves, finely chopped

Sprig of thyme, leaves only,
 chopped

Sprig of rosemary, leaves only,
 chopped

1 Tbsp kosher salt

1 tsp black pepper

2 Tbsp Potato Seasoning
 (see here)

1 Tbsp butter, diced

**POTATO SEASONING**  Combine all ingredients in a small bowl. Store at room temperature for up to 1 week.

**BRUNCH POTATOES**  Preheat oven to 350°F.

Prepare a medium bowl of ice water. Peel potatoes and cut into ½-inch cubes. As you are working, place potatoes in ice water to prevent browning and remove excess starch. Rinse potatoes until water runs clear and pat-dry.

Heat oil in a large ovenproof skillet over medium-high heat. Add potatoes and pan-fry on all sides for 5–6 minutes, until golden brown. Add onion and bell pepper and cook for 2 minutes. Stir in garlic, thyme, rosemary, salt, black pepper, potato seasoning, and butter.

Place the skillet in the oven and roast for 5 minutes, until potatoes are cooked but not mushy.

Store in the fridge for up to 3 days or freeze for up to 1 month. When ready to serve, thaw at room temperature and then crisp in a skillet.

> **NOTE**  If you want to prepare potatoes in advance, peel and dice them as instructed. Then, place potatoes in ice water to prevent browning and remove excess starch. When ready to use, rinse potatoes until water runs clear and pat-dry.

# CARNITAS HASH

**SERVES 2**

**NF**

This is the one that made me famous. I love making carnitas, and this is the first hash I made when we opened Hash Kitchen. I put it all together, and we tasted it and said, "Oh my God, it works. It's perfect."

## FRIED ONIONS

1 cup buttermilk
2 red onions, thinly sliced
2 cups canola oil
1 cup all-purpose flour
1 Tbsp cornstarch
1 Tbsp smoked paprika
1 tsp kosher salt
½ tsp garlic powder
½ tsp black pepper

## CARNITAS HASH

5 tsp canola or olive oil
(divided)
2 cups Carnitas (page 139)
4 cups Brunch Potatoes
(page 108)
¼ cup fresh corn kernels
4 eggs
Kosher salt and black pepper
1 avocado, for garnish
¾ cup Salsa Verde (page 166)
4 corn tortillas, warmed
2 cups Fried Onions (see here),
for garnish
2 Tbsp chopped cilantro,
for garnish
1 Tbsp grated Cotija cheese,
for garnish
2 Tbsp sour cream, for garnish

**FRIED ONIONS** In a medium bowl, combine buttermilk and onions. Marinate for at least 10 minutes or overnight.

Heat oil in a deep skillet over medium-high heat until it reaches a temperature of 350°F.

In a large bowl, place flour, cornstarch, and spices and whisk until combined.

Drain onions, then evenly coat in the flour mixture. Carefully lower onions into the hot oil and fry for 2 minutes, until golden brown and crispy. Using a slotted spoon, transfer to a paper towel–lined plate to drain excess oil. Set aside.

**CARNITAS HASH** Heat 1 tablespoon of oil in a large cast-iron skillet over medium-high heat. Add carnitas and sauté for 3–4 minutes, until heated through. Place in a medium bowl and cover to keep warm.

Heat the residual oil from the carnitas in the same skillet over medium-high heat. Add potatoes and corn and cook for 3 minutes, until hot.

Heat the remaining 2 teaspoons of oil in an 8-inch skillet over medium heat. Add eggs and fry for 2½ minutes for sunny-side-up (or to your desired doneness). Season with salt and pepper.

Meanwhile, halve avocado and remove the pit. Thinly slice each half, fanning out the slices.

To serve, divide the potatoes between two plates. Top each with carnitas and salsa. Place eggs and tortillas on top, then garnish with fried onions, avocado, cilantro, Cotija, and sour cream.

# SHORT RIB POUTINE HASH

**SERVES 2**

**NF**

Poutine is a popular Canadian dish that typically consists of French fries and cheese curds covered in hot gravy. I had a Canadian friend who ordered it, and we were all laughing at the name. But then, I had it and wondered how I'd make it better. Here, we "Chef Joey" it up with braised short ribs and mozzarella and smother everything with rich brown demi gravy.

### BROWN DEMI GRAVY

2 Tbsp butter

2 Tbsp all-purpose flour

1 cup beef stock

1 cup chicken stock

1 tsp chopped thyme

1 tsp granulated garlic

½ tsp kosher salt

1 tsp heavy cream

### SHORT RIB POUTINE HASH

1 Tbsp canola or olive oil

4 cups French fries

4 oz mini mozzarella balls (bocconcini), cut into ½-inch chunks

2 cups Braised Short Ribs (page 138)

4 eggs

2 Tbsp white vinegar

2 scallions, for garnish

Kosher salt and black pepper

¾ cup Brown Demi Gravy (see here), warmed

2 Tbsp finely chopped chives, for garnish

**BROWN DEMI GRAVY**  Melt butter in a heavy saucepan over medium heat. Slowly add flour, whisking constantly, until the roux is lightly golden and smells like popcorn. Do not brown. Set aside.

In a medium saucepan, combine stocks, thyme, garlic, salt, and cream. Whisk in the roux and bring to a boil. Reduce heat to medium-low and simmer until the mixture is thick enough to coat the back of a spoon.

The gravy can be stored in the fridge for 1 week or frozen for up to 3 months.

**SHORT RIB POUTINE HASH**  Preheat oven to 350°F.

Heat oil in a large ovenproof skillet over medium-high heat. Add fries and cook for 3 minutes, until hot. Top with mozzarella. Bake for 1–2 minutes, until cheese has melted.

Add short ribs and bake for another 5 minutes.

Bring a medium saucepan of water to a boil.

Meanwhile, crack an egg into a fine-mesh sieve over a small bowl. Gently swirl the egg in the sieve so that the loose, watery egg white drains into the bowl. Place the intact egg in a separate small bowl. Repeat with the remaining eggs.

Stir vinegar into the boiling water, creating a vortex by vigorously stirring the water in a circle. Add an egg to the middle of the vortex and cook for 3 minutes. Using a slotted spoon, transfer egg to a paper towel–lined plate to drain excess water. Repeat with the remaining eggs.

Heat a medium sauté pan over high heat. Add scallions and cook on each side for 1 minute, until lightly charred.

To serve, divide short rib hash between two plates. Top each with two eggs. Season eggs with salt and pepper. Garnish each plate with 1 scallion. Pour gravy on top. Garnish with chives.

# SMOKED BRISKET
# *and* CORNBREAD HASH

SERVES 2

I used to own a barbecue restaurant, and I'd smoke meat all the time. Brisket is one of those cuts that I fell in love with. And you can't have hash without potatoes, right? So I added them to the cornbread, and it was frickin' delicious! The breakfast flavors with the sweetness of the cornbread and the spice of the brisket rub work incredibly together.

## CORNBREAD
Cooking spray
½ cup (63 g) all-purpose flour
½ cup (78 g) yellow cornmeal
⅓ cup (67 g) granulated sugar
1¾ tsp (9 g) baking powder
½ tsp (3 g) kosher salt
1¼ cups (2½ sticks, 284 g) butter, melted
½ cup (123 g) whole milk
1 egg (50 g), beaten
2 cups (284 g) Brunch Potatoes (page 108)

## HASH
5 tsp canola or olive oil (divided)
4 slices Smoked Brisket (page 177), cut ¼-inch thick
4 eggs
Kosher salt and black pepper
Cornbread (see here)
½ cup Chef Pierce Hollandaise (page 169)
2 Tbsp thinly sliced chives
2 cups Fried Onions (page 109 [Carnitas Hash])

**CORNBREAD**  Preheat oven to 400°F. Grease a 9-inch round or square baking pan or cast-iron pan with cooking spray.

In a medium bowl, place flour, cornmeal, sugar, baking powder, and salt. Whisk to combine.

Make a well in the center of the dry ingredients. Add butter, milk, and egg and stir until the mixture comes together and a few lumps remain. Pour the batter into the prepared pan. Bake for 10 minutes.

Place potatoes randomly in the batter and bake for another 10–15 minutes, until the top is a deep golden brown and a toothpick inserted into the center comes out clean.

**HASH**  Heat 1 tablespoon of oil in a large skillet over medium-high heat. Add brisket slices and cook for 2 minutes on each side, until hot throughout. Place the brisket slices on a plate and cover to keep warm.

Meanwhile, heat the remaining 2 teaspoons of oil in an 8-inch skillet over medium heat. Add eggs and cook for 2½ minutes for sunny-side-up (or to your desired doneness). Season with salt and pepper.

To serve, divide the cornbread mixture between two plates. Top each with two brisket slices and two eggs. Pour hollandaise over eggs. Top with chives and fried onions.

# BEST F#*%ING BIRRIA HASH

This birria hash became an instant favorite on our menu. Crisp brunch potatoes are topped with tender, juicy beef, poached eggs with hollandaise, sharp onions, and vibrant cilantro. Served with quesadillas and warm consommé, it's a great dish for entertaining.

2 cups Birria (page 141)

1 cup Consommé (page 141)

1 Tbsp canola or olive oil

4 cups Brunch Potatoes (page 108)

¼ cup fresh corn kernels

6 (5-inch) corn tortillas

2 cups shredded mozzarella
 (divided)

4 eggs

2 Tbsp white vinegar

Kosher salt and black pepper

¼ cup Chef Pierce Hollandaise
 (page 169)

½ tsp smoked paprika

1 white onion, chopped, for garnish

¼ cup chopped cilantro, for garnish

2 cups Fried Onions (page 109
 [Carnitas Hash]), for garnish

Combine birria and consommé in a large skillet over medium-high heat. Heat for 3 minutes, until warmed through.

Strain consommé into a medium bowl. Put birria in another medium bowl. Keep both warm.

Heat oil in the same skillet over medium-high heat. Add potatoes and corn kernels and cook for 3 minutes, until hot.

Meanwhile, dip a few tortillas into consommé and place in a 10-inch skillet over medium heat. Cook for 1 minute, then top each with ⅓ cup mozzarella. Carefully fold tortillas in half. Continue to cook for another minute per side, until cheese is melted. Transfer quesadillas to a plate. Repeat with the remaining tortillas.

Bring a medium saucepan of water to a boil.

Meanwhile, crack an egg into a fine-mesh sieve over a small bowl. Gently swirl the egg in the sieve so that the loose, watery egg white drains into the bowl. Place the intact egg in a separate small bowl. Repeat with the remaining eggs.

Stir vinegar into the boiling water, creating a vortex by vigorously stirring the water in a circle. Add an egg to the middle of the vortex and cook for 3 minutes. Using a slotted spoon, transfer egg to a paper towel–lined plate to drain excess water. Repeat with the remaining eggs.

Divide potatoes between two plates. Place eggs in the center, with birria on one side and quesadillas on the other. Season eggs with salt and pepper and top with hollandaise and paprika. Garnish with white onion and cilantro between eggs and quesadillas. Garnish with fried onions between birria and eggs. Serve with ramekins of warm consommé.

# HUEVOS RANCHEROS HASH

**SERVES 2**

**NF**

Huevos rancheros was a popular morning staff meal. The guys would say, "Hey, boss! Can we have some steaks?" I'd laugh and pull out the filet mignon, and we'd have huevos rancheros. It was a delicious way to start the day.

Huevos rancheros are traditionally served as fried eggs on top of corn tortillas with a chile-spiked tomato sauce. I've transformed this dish into an amazing hash with juicy carne asada.

**CARNE ASADA**

2 Tbsp canola oil

¼ cup orange juice

1 Tbsp lime juice

2 Tbsp paprika

1 tsp garlic powder

1 tsp onion powder

1 tsp ground cumin

12 oz skirt steak

**HUEVOS RANCHEROS HASH**

2 Tbsp + 2 tsp canola or olive oil (divided)

Carne Asada (see here)

4 cups Brunch Potatoes (page 108)

4 eggs

Kosher salt and black pepper

1 avocado

4 scallions

2 store-bought tostadas

1 cup canned black beans, rinsed and drained

¾ cup Salsa Rojo (page 165)

¾ cup Salsa Verde (page 166)

1 tsp Tajin

Grated Cotija cheese, for garnish

2 Tbsp sour cream

Chopped cilantro, for garnish

**CARNE ASADA**  In a medium bowl, combine all ingredients except steak. Mix until fully combined. Add steak, coat in marinade, and refrigerate for at least 4 hours to marinate.

**HUEVOS RANCHEROS HASH**  Heat 1 tablespoon of oil in a large cast-iron skillet over medium-high heat. Remove steak from marinade. Add steak to the skillet and sear for 2 minutes on each side for medium-rare. Transfer to a cutting board and set aside to rest for at least 5 minutes.

Heat 1 tablespoon of oil in the same skillet. Add potatoes and cook for 3 minutes, until hot. Keep warm.

Meanwhile, heat the remaining 2 teaspoons of oil in an 8-inch skillet over medium heat. Add eggs and fry for 2½ minutes for sunny-side-up (or to your desired doneness). Season with salt and pepper.

Slice steak. Halve avocado and remove the pit. Thinly slice each half, fanning out the slices.

Heat a medium sauté pan over high heat. Add scallions and cook on each side for 1 minute, until lightly charred.

Divide potatoes among two plates and top with steak. Place tostada beside steak. Top steak with black beans, eggs, scallions, avocado, and salsas. Sprinkle Tajin over eggs and tostada. Garnish with Cotija. Drizzle with sour cream and garnish with cilantro.

# GNOCCHI CARBONARA HASH

**SERVES 4**

Carbonara reminds me of my childhood. I was just eight years old when I had carbonara for the first time, with my dad, at a restaurant in Sicily. The sun was shining, the air was warm, and the pasta was delicious.

Gnocchi, like hash, are made from potatoes. To make perfect gnocchi, create a smooth and silky dough by using finely milled "oo" flour. We add English peas, pancetta, and some cream for the American palate. With an egg on top, it's a fun and tasty brunch dish with an Italian flair.

**GNOCCHI**

2 lbs Yukon Gold or Kennebec potatoes, unpeeled

2 Tbsp + 1 tsp kosher salt (divided)

2½ cups "oo" flour, plus extra for dusting

⅛ tsp ground nutmeg

2 eggs

**GNOCCHI**  Combine potatoes and 2 tablespoons of salt in a stockpot. Add enough water to cover the potatoes and bring to a boil. Boil for 20 minutes, until fork tender. Drain, then set aside until cool enough to handle.

Halve potatoes lengthwise, then remove the skin. While still warm, pass potatoes through a ricer set over a medium bowl. (Alternatively, push potatoes through a mesh strainer.) Lightly sprinkle flour, nutmeg, and the remaining teaspoon of salt over potatoes. Mix well until no longer sticky.

Make a well in the center of the potato mixture and crack eggs into the well. Whisk eggs with a fork, then work the mixture with your hands until a dough ball forms.

On a clean surface lightly dusted with flour, divide the ball into 4 equal portions. Roll each dough piece into a log, about ¾-inch in diameter. With a knife, cut the dough into 1-inch segments.

Gnocchi can be dusted with flour and stored in the fridge for up to 1 day. To freeze, space out gnocchi on a baking sheet and freeze until firm. Transfer to a freezer-proof container or zip-top bag and freeze for up to 1 month.

*continued*

## GNOCCHI CARBONARA HASH

1 Tbsp kosher salt, plus extra
  for seasoning
5 tsp canola or olive oil (divided)
4 cups Brunch Potatoes (page 108)
½ cup diced pancetta
1 shallot, finely chopped
1 cup heavy cream
½ cup frozen peas
2 Tbsp grated Parmesan,
  plus extra for garnish
Black pepper
2 cups Gnocchi (see here)
4 eggs

**GNOCCHI CARBONARA HASH** Bring 6 cups salted water to a boil in a large pot over high heat.

Meanwhile, heat 1 tablespoon of oil in a large cast-iron skillet over medium-high heat. Add potatoes and cook for 3 minutes, until hot. Keep warm.

Add pancetta to a 10-inch skillet and sauté over medium heat for 5 minutes, until golden brown. Using a slotted spoon, transfer pancetta to a paper towel–lined plate to drain excess oil.

Add shallot to the same skillet and sauté in the pancetta fat for 1 minute, until translucent. Add cream, peas, Parmesan, pepper, and pancetta and cook for 5–6 minutes, until sauce thickens enough to coat the back of a spoon. Turn off the heat.

Add gnocchi to boiling water and cook for 4–5 minutes, until they float to the surface. Using a slotted spoon, remove from water and place into the skillet with the cream mixture.

Meanwhile, heat the remaining 2 teaspoons of oil in an 8-inch skillet over medium heat. Add eggs and fry for 2½ minutes for sunny-side-up (or to your desired doneness). Season with salt and pepper.

To serve, divide potatoes among four plates. Top with the gnocchi and panchetta mixture and eggs. Garnish with Parmesan.

# BLUE CRAB
## *and* SWEET POTATO HASH

SERVES 2

NF

I wanted to create a light, new version of the hearty hash. The sweetness of the crabmeat goes well with the sweet potatoes, and the creamy hollandaise with Old Bay, a classic seafood seasoning blend, ties everything together.

**OLD BAY HOLLANDAISE**

6 egg yolks
2 Tbsp lemon juice
½ tsp Old Bay Seasoning
1 cup (2 sticks) butter, melted
Kosher salt, to taste

**BLUE CRAB AND SWEET POTATO HASH**

1 Tbsp olive or canola oil
2 large sweet potatoes,
  coarsely shredded with a
  box grater
1 tsp kosher salt, plus extra
  for seasoning
½ tsp black pepper, plus extra
  for seasoning
4 eggs
2 Tbsp white vinegar
1 Tbsp butter
8 oz lump blue crabmeat
¼ cup Old Bay Hollandaise
  (see here)
1 Tbsp finely chopped chives
1 tsp Old Bay Seasoning
Fried Onions (page 109
  [Carnitas Hash]), for garnish

**OLD BAY HOLLANDAISE**  Combine egg yolks, lemon juice, and Old Bay in a blender and blend on high speed for 30 seconds.

With the motor still running, slowly pour in butter in a thin and steady stream until the mixture is creamy and smooth. Season with salt. Use immediately.

**BLUE CRAB AND SWEET POTATO HASH**  Heat oil in a large skillet over medium-high heat. Add sweet potatoes, salt, and pepper and mix. Fry for 3–4 minutes, untouched, until potatoes begin to brown and crisp on the edges. Flip potatoes and cook for another 3 minutes.

Bring a medium saucepan of water to a boil.

Meanwhile, crack an egg into a fine-mesh sieve over a small bowl. Gently swirl the egg in the sieve so that the loose, watery egg white drains into the bowl. Place the intact egg in a separate small bowl. Repeat with the remaining eggs.

Stir vinegar into the boiling water, creating a vortex by vigorously stirring the water in a circle. Add an egg to the middle of the vortex and cook for 3 minutes. Using a slotted spoon, transfer egg to a paper towel–lined plate to drain excess water. Repeat with the remaining eggs.

Melt butter in a small skillet. Add crab and gently warm for 3 minutes. Remove from heat.

To serve, spread potatoes evenly onto each plate. Place the crab mixture in the center of the dish and surround it with eggs. Season eggs with salt and pepper. Top with hollandaise and chives. Sprinkle with Old Bay seasoning. Garnish with fried onions and serve immediately.

# BLACKENED SHRIMP *and* GRITS HASH

While shrimp and grits can be eaten all day long, I find it's perfect for breakfast and brunch. But when it comes to the grits, my version is made with polenta and creamy mascarpone. What can I say? I'm Italian.

**BLACKENING SEASONING**

2 Tbsp paprika

1 Tbsp cayenne powder

1 Tbsp onion powder

1 Tbsp garlic powder

1 tsp black pepper

1 tsp kosher salt

½ tsp dried basil

½ tsp dried oregano

½ tsp dried thyme

**MASCARPONE POLENTA**

2 cups whole milk

1 tsp kosher salt

2 cups chicken stock

1 cup coarse yellow polenta

2 Tbsp butter

3 Tbsp mascarpone

**BLACKENING SEASONING** In a small bowl, combine all ingredients and mix thoroughly.

**MASCARPONE POLENTA** In a large saucepan, combine milk, salt, and stock. Heat over medium-high heat until the mixture begins to steam. Slowly whisk in polenta. Reduce heat to medium-low and cook for 15 minutes, stirring occasionally.

Reduce heat to low. Stir in butter until melted and fully incorporated. Turn off the heat, then fold in mascarpone and mix until creamy and smooth.

*continued*

2 cups Mascarpone Polenta
(see here)

½ cup whole milk

2 Tbsp olive or canola oil
(divided)

4 cups Brunch Potatoes
(page 108)

8 (U-15) shrimp, deveined
and tail-on

1 tsp Blackening Seasoning
(see here)

½ tsp kosher salt, plus extra
for seasoning

4 eggs

2 Tbsp white vinegar

Black pepper

2 sprigs thyme, for garnish

2 Tbsp thinly sliced chives,
for garnish

**ASSEMBLY**  Combine polenta and milk in a 10-inch saucepan and heat over medium heat until hot. (Polenta will thicken up as it cools, so it needs more liquid to be thinned out when rewarming.)

Heat 1 tablespoon of oil in a large cast-iron skillet over medium-high heat. Add potatoes and cook for 3 minutes, until hot. Transfer to a medium bowl and cover to keep warm.

In a small bowl, combine shrimp, blackening seasoning, and salt and stir well to evenly coat.

Heat the remaining tablespoon of oil in the same skillet over medium heat. Add shrimp and cook for 2 minutes. Flip, then cook for another 2 minutes. Transfer shrimp to a plate, then set aside.

Bring a medium saucepan of water to a boil.

Meanwhile, crack an egg into a fine-mesh sieve over a bowl. Gently swirl the egg in the sieve so that the loose, watery egg white drains into the bowl. Place the intact egg in a separate small bowl. Repeat with the remaining eggs.

Stir vinegar into the boiling water, creating a vortex by vigorously stirring the water in a circle. Add an egg to the middle of the vortex and cook for 3 minutes. Using a slotted spoon, transfer egg to a paper towel–lined plate to drain excess water. Repeat with the remaining eggs.

To serve, divide polenta between two bowls. Top with potatoes and eggs. Season eggs with salt and pepper. Top with shrimp. Garnish with thyme and chives.

# OVER-THE-TOP Signature DISHES BY AN OVER-THE-TOP Chef.

# CHEF JOEY'S BRUNCH LIFE

# BILLIONAIRE'S BACON

**MAKES 8 SLICES**

**DF** **NF**

Now, this is how you do bacon. Brush thick-cut slices with maple-yuzu glaze, spiced brown sugar, and luxurious gold leaf.

**MAPLE-YUZU GLAZE**
2½ cups maple syrup
¾ cup soy sauce
¼ tsp ground allspice
1 Tbsp yuzu juice (see Note)

**BROWN SUGAR–CHILI RUB**
1 cup packed brown sugar
1 Tbsp chili flakes

**ASSEMBLY**
8 thick-cut strips applewood
 smoked bacon
Maple-Yuzu Glaze (see here)
Brown Sugar–Chili Rub (see here),
 for sprinkling
Edible gold leaf flakes,
 for garnish (see Note)

**MAPLE-YUZU GLAZE** Place all ingredients in a small saucepan and whisk to combine. Simmer over medium heat for 10–15 minutes, until the mixture is thick enough to coat the back of a spoon. Whisk continuously to prevent scorching.

> **NOTE** Yuzu is an aromatic citrus native to Asia. Bottled juice is more readily available than fresh fruit and is available from Asian markets, specialty grocers, and online sources.

**BROWN SUGAR–CHILI RUB** Combine all ingredients in a small bowl and mix thoroughly.

**ASSEMBLY** Preheat oven to 350°F. Place a wire rack over a baking sheet to cook the bacon. (If you don't have a wire rack, line the baking sheet with parchment paper.)

Arrange bacon in a single layer on the wire rack. Grill for 10 minutes. Turn slices over and grill for another 7–9 minutes, until crispy.

While still hot, brush each bacon slice with maple-yuzu glaze and sprinkle with sugar rub.

When ready to serve, garnish with gold leaf flakes for that billionaire's touch!

> **NOTE** Edible gold leaf can be purchased in sheets or flakes, though flakes are easier to handle. Look for jars of flakes at cake and candy decorating shops and on Amazon.

# FRIED CHICKEN

**SERVES 2**

**NF**

This juicy fried chicken is delicious on its own, but it's especially tasty with biscuits for Fried Chicken Benedict (page 86) or when paired with maple syrup and crispy waffles (page 80).

**BUTTERMILK-BRINED CHICKEN**

2 boneless, skin-on chicken breasts
4 cups buttermilk
1 cup pickle juice

**CHICKEN FLOUR**

1 cup all-purpose flour
1 Tbsp paprika
1 Tbsp kosher salt
1 tsp garlic powder
1 tsp onion powder
1 tsp black pepper
½ tsp ground cumin
½ tsp cayenne powder

**ASSEMBLY**

4 cups canola oil
Buttermilk-Brined Chicken (see here)
Chicken Flour (see here)

**BUTTERMILK-BRINED CHICKEN** Using a mallet, pound chicken to about 1-inch thick.

In a large bowl, mix buttermilk and pickle juice. Add chicken and press down to fully submerge. Cover with plastic wrap and brine in the fridge for at least 12 hours and up to 36 hours.

**CHICKEN FLOUR** Place all ingredients in a medium bowl and whisk until combined.

**ASSEMBLY** Heat oil in a deep saucepan over medium-high heat until it reaches a temperature of 350°F.

Remove chicken from buttermilk brine. Dredge in chicken flour, pressing firmly to ensure chicken is fully coated. Carefully lower chicken into the hot oil and deep-fry for 5 minutes, until the internal temperature reaches 165°F. Using tongs, transfer to a wire resting rack to drain excess oil and keep chicken skin crispy.

# HASH AVOCADO TOAST

**SERVES 2**
**NF**

People tend to eat avocado toast for health reasons, so I created it to be sexy and amazing. With carnitas, bacon, and green chile hollandaise, this big, meaty avocado toast has mega flavor.

**FRIED LEEKS**

2 cups canola oil

1 cup all-purpose flour

1 Tbsp smoked paprika

1 tsp kosher salt

½ tsp garlic powder

½ tsp black pepper

1 large leek, white and light green parts only, thinly sliced

**HASH AVOCADO TOAST**

2 Tbsp olive oil (divided)

2 cups Carnitas (page 139)

2 Tbsp butter

4 slices brioche bread, about 2 inches thick

4 eggs

Kosher salt and black pepper

2 large avocados

4 strips cooked bacon

½ cup Green Chile Hollandaise (page 170)

2 cups Fried Leeks (see here)

**FRIED LEEKS** Heat oil in a deep skillet over medium-high heat until it reaches a temperature of 350°F.

In a medium bowl, combine flour, paprika, salt, garlic, and pepper and whisk.

Dredge leek in the flour mixture, shaking off excess. Carefully lower leek into the hot oil and deep-fry for 1 minute, until golden brown and crispy. Using a slotted spoon, transfer leek to a paper towel–lined plate to drain excess oil.

**HASH AVOCADO TOAST** Heat 1 tablespoon of oil in a large skillet over medium-high heat. Add carnitas and sauté for 3–4 minutes, until warmed through. Transfer to a medium bowl and cover with a dish towel to keep warm.

Melt butter in the same skillet over medium-high heat. Add brioche and fry for 2 minutes on each side, until golden brown. Set aside.

Heat 2 teaspoons of oil in the same skillet over medium heat. Add eggs and fry for 2½ minutes for sunny-side-up (or to your desired doneness). Season with salt and pepper.

Meanwhile, pit and chop avocados. In a small bowl, combine avocados and the remaining teaspoon of oil and mix well, keeping the mixture on the chunkier side. Season with salt and pepper.

Place two slices of toast on each plate. Spread avocado over toast, then add carnitas, bacon, and eggs. Pour hollandaise on top. Top with fried leeks.

# HASH AVOCADO TOAST p. 135

# BRAISED SHORT RIBS

**SERVES 4**

Braised short ribs remind me of Italian sugo, where the meat is cooked for hours. They're easy, forgiving to cook, and very versatile. You can add them to a lot of the recipes throughout the book; you could make short ribs with grits or polenta, short rib tacos, or short rib frittata. And they're even better the next day.

3 lbs beef short ribs
1 Tbsp kosher salt
1 tsp black pepper
2 Tbsp canola oil
12 garlic cloves, smashed
1 small white onion, chopped
  (½ cup)
½ medium fennel bulb,
  cored and chopped (⅓ cup)
1 small carrot, chopped
  (⅓ cup)
2 bay leaves
Sprig of rosemary
Sprig of thyme
1 (750-mL) bottle red wine
  (preferably Zinfandel)
2 cups chicken stock
1 (8-oz can) whole peeled
  tomatoes, hand crushed

Preheat oven to 350°F.

Pat-dry short ribs. Season with salt and pepper.

Heat an ovenproof Dutch oven over medium-high heat until hot. Add oil, then arrange short ribs in the pan and sear for 3–4 minutes, until brown and crusty on all sides. Transfer to a plate and set aside.

To the same Dutch oven, add garlic, onion, fennel, carrot, bay leaves, rosemary, and thyme. Sauté for 5 minutes over medium-high heat until fragrant and onion is softened. Add short ribs, wine, stock, and tomatoes. Cover, then cook in the oven for 4 hours, until short ribs are fork tender.

Transfer short ribs to a cutting board and set aside. Remove bay leaves from the hot braising liquid. Using an immersion blender, blend braising liquid until smooth. Return ribs to the Dutch oven. Serve immediately.

Leftover ribs can be stored in an airtight container in the fridge for up to 5 days.

# CARNITAS

**MAKES 10 LBS**

**DF** **NF**

I have a passion for Mexican food (we're in Arizona, after all!) and have been cooking it at home for twenty years. I always like the combination of Coke syrup and pork belly, so I thought I'd try the same with carnitas.

Delicious with eggs and tortillas, this staple is great for breakfast or dinner. Although it's easy to make, it does require time to prepare. Don't let that dissuade you—the payoff is amazing.

1 (10-lb) pork butt, fat trimmed and reserved
⅓ cup pork fat
12 garlic cloves, smashed
1 large yellow onion, quartered
⅓ cup kosher salt
1 Tbsp black pepper
1½ tsp dried Mexican oregano (see Note)
⅓ tsp ground cumin
4 cups chicken stock
1 cup Coca-Cola

Melt reserved fat trimmings and pork fat in a Dutch oven over medium heat. Add pork butt, which should be three-quarters submerged. Add the remaining ingredients. Cover, then refrigerate for at least 12 hours.

Preheat oven to 350°F.

Cover the Dutch oven with a lid (or baking sheet wrapped in aluminum foil). Braise for 3½ hours, until pork is fork tender.

Transfer pork to a cutting board, reserving braising liquid. Using two forks, shred pork. Spoon over some braising liquid to moisten the meat. Reserve the remainder.

Meat and braising liquid can be stored separately in airtight containers in the fridge for up to 5 days or frozen for up to 3 months.

> **NOTE** Mexican oregano is native to Mexico and Central America and has a more robust flavor than Italian or Greek oregano. Look for Mexican oregano in the dried spices section or the Mexican/Asian food aisle in grocery stores.

# BIRRIA *and* CONSOMMÉ

SERVES 4–6

GF  DF  NF

Originating from the state of Jalisco in Mexico, birria is slow-cooked beef or goat braised with chiles and rich spices. The resultant juices are served alongside as a vibrant consommé. And because the broth has so much flavor, almost anything dunked in it will taste incredible—you can't go wrong.

1 (2½-lb) chuck roast

1 Tbsp kosher salt

3 garlic cloves, chopped

2 Roma tomatoes, chopped

1 dried mulato pepper, stemmed and seeded (see Note)

1 dried guajillo pepper, stemmed and seeded

1 white onion, chopped

½ tsp ground cumin

½ tsp black pepper

¼ tsp ground cinnamon

¼ tsp dried Mexican oregano (see Note)

Bring 1½ gallons water to a boil in a stockpot. Add chuck roast and salt.

Meanwhile, combine the remaining ingredients in a blender. Pour in 1 cup water and blend until smooth. Stir the mixture into the pot. Reduce heat to medium-low and simmer, uncovered, for 3½ hours, until beef is fork tender.

Transfer beef to a cutting board, reserving consommé. Using two forks, shred beef, discarding any large pieces of fat. Spoon over some consommé to moisten the meat. Reserve the remainder.

Meat and consommé can be stored separately in airtight containers in the fridge for up to 5 days or frozen for up to 3 months.

> **NOTE** The mulato pepper is a dried, matured poblano pepper. Mulato peppers can be purchased at Latin food stores or online. Mexican oregano is native to Mexico and Central America and has a more robust flavor than Italian or Greek oregano. Look for Mexican oregano in the dried spices section or the Mexican/Asian food aisle in grocery stores.

# CHILAQUILES

Chilaquiles goes back to my time in Southern California. I would drive up from San Diego and hit a little place in Manhattan Beach for a chilaquiles burrito. Back then, I had no idea what it was except that it was delicious.

We added chicken tinga to this more traditional recipe, but you can also make it with any of the meats, like Braised Short Ribs (page 138), Carnitas (page 139), or Birria (page 141).

### CHICKEN

2½ lbs boneless, skinless chicken breast
½ white onion, chopped
2 garlic cloves, smashed
1 Tbsp kosher salt
½ Tbsp black peppercorns

### TINGA

4 Roma tomatoes
4 dried Morita chiles, stemmed and seeded
4 garlic cloves, chopped
1 white onion, chopped
1 (4-oz) can chipotle peppers in adobo
⅓ cup tomato paste
1 Tbsp kosher salt
1 cup reserved braising liquid (see here), plus extra if needed

### ASSEMBLY

1 Tbsp + 2 tsp olive or canola oil (divided)
2 cups Chicken Tinga (see here)
4 cups corn tortilla chips
2 cups Salsa Verde (page 166)
4 eggs
Kosher salt and black pepper
2 Tbsp sour cream, for garnish
2 tsp grated Cotija cheese, for garnish
2 tsp chopped cilantro, for garnish

**CHICKEN** Combine all ingredients in a large saucepan. Add enough water to cover and bring to a boil over high heat. Reduce heat to medium and simmer for 15–25 minutes, until chicken is tender and cooked through.

Transfer chicken to a cutting board, reserving braising liquid. Using two forks, shred chicken and cover it. Set aside.

**TINGA** Combine all ingredients in a blender and blend until the mixture is smooth and thick enough to coat the back of a spoon. If too thick, add more braising liquid.

Pour the mixture into a medium saucepan. Add shredded chicken and simmer for 20 minutes over medium heat, stirring occasionally.

Chicken can be stored in the fridge for up to 5 days or frozen for up to 3 months.

**ASSEMBLY** Heat 1 tablespoon of oil in a large skillet over medium heat. Add chicken tinga and cook for 2–3 minutes, until hot. Place in a medium bowl and keep warm.

Add tortilla chips and salsa to the skillet. Stir to evenly coat chips and cook for 3 minutes.

Meanwhile, heat the remaining 2 teaspoons of oil in an 8-inch skillet over medium heat. Add eggs and fry for 2½ minutes for sunny-side-up (or to your desired doneness). Season with salt and pepper.

Divide the chilaquiles into two bowls. Top each with chicken tinga and two eggs. Garnish with sour cream, Cotija, and cilantro.

# Maso's
# BREAKFAST POTATO TACOS

**SERVES 2**

**VEG** **NF**

We used to have a woman named Lupe who worked for us and remains a close family friend. My kids loved her potato tacos, especially my son, Tomaso, so these were inspired by those tacos and named after him.

They're great when you need to feed a large crowd, because they can be prepared in advance and served at room temperature.

### POTATO TACOS

2 large russet potatoes, peeled and cut into 2-inch cubes

1 Tbsp kosher salt

½ tsp black pepper

½ cup shredded mozzarella

1 cup canola oil

8 (5-inch) corn tortillas

### BREAKFAST POTATO TACOS

2 tsp olive or canola oil

4 eggs

Kosher salt and black pepper

Potato Tacos (see here)

2 cups shredded iceberg lettuce

½ cup diced tomatoes

½ cup Salsa Verde (page 166)

2 Tbsp grated Cotija cheese, for garnish

2 Tbsp chopped cilantro, for garnish

**POTATO TACOS** Place potatoes in a medium saucepan and cover with water. Bring to a boil over medium-high heat. Reduce heat to medium-low and simmer for 15–20 minutes, until fork tender.

Drain potatoes, then place in a medium bowl. Pass through a ricer or mash with a fork. Season with salt and pepper, then fold in mozzarella and mix until fully incorporated.

Heat oil in a deep skillet over medium-high heat. Carefully add tortillas to the hot oil and cook for 10 seconds on each side, until softened. Using tongs, transfer to a paper towel–lined plate to drain excess oil.

Place 1 tablespoon of potato filling in a tortilla. Press to close. Carefully lower the filled tacos into the hot oil and fry for 2 minutes, until golden brown and crispy.

**BREAKFAST POTATO TACOS** Heat oil in an 8-inch skillet over medium heat. Add eggs and fry for 2½ minutes for sunny-side-up (or to your desired doneness). Season with salt and pepper.

To serve, place four potato tacos on each plate. Top with lettuce, tomatoes, salsa, and two eggs. Garnish with Cotija and cilantro.

# *Ten-Layer* BREAKFAST LASAGNA

My daughter Melina loves traditional lasagna, so I wanted to make something she could enjoy for breakfast. We reinvented this beautiful Italian signature dish for brunch with the addition of bacon and fried eggs.

## BÉCHAMEL

1 Tbsp butter
1 Tbsp all-purpose flour
2 cups whole milk
1 cup heavy cream
½ tsp kosher salt
¼ tsp ground nutmeg
Pinch of white pepper

## SAUSAGE RAGU

1 Tbsp olive oil
1 small white onion, chopped (½ cup)
1 small carrot, chopped (⅓ cup)
1 small fennel bulb, chopped (⅓ cup)
1 lb ground Italian sausage
1 Tbsp kosher salt
1 tsp black pepper
2 bay leaves
1 Tbsp tomato paste
1 (750-mL) bottle red wine (preferably Zinfandel)
1 (28-oz) can whole peeled tomatoes

**BÉCHAMEL** Melt butter in a heavy saucepan over medium heat. Slowly add flour, whisking constantly, until the roux is lightly golden and smells like popcorn. Do not brown. Set aside.

Combine milk and cream in a large saucepan and bring to a boil over medium heat. Whisk in salt, nutmeg, and pepper. Add the roux and whisk continuously.

Reduce heat to low. Whisk for 2 minutes, until smooth and silky. Remove from heat once the sauce coats the back of a spoon, then set aside.

Béchamel can be stored in an airtight container in the fridge for up to 4 days.

**SAUSAGE RAGU** Heat oil in a large saucepan over medium-high heat. Add onion, carrot, and fennel and sauté for 7 minutes, until translucent.

Add sausage, salt, and pepper and sauté for 10 minutes, until sausage is crumbled and browned. Stir in bay leaves and tomato paste. Cook for another 2 minutes.

Pour in wine and simmer for 10–15 minutes, until the liquid is reduced by half. Add tomatoes, breaking them up with a wooden spoon. Reduce heat to medium and simmer for 1 hour, stirring occasionally. Remove bay leaves.

Cooking spray

1 Tbsp kosher salt, plus extra
for seasoning

10 lasagna sheets

2¾ cups Sausage Ragu
(see here)

3½ cups Béchamel
(divided, see here)

2 cups whole milk ricotta
(such as Polly-O)

1 cup grated Parmesan,
plus extra for garnish

2½ cups shredded whole
milk mozzarella

8 strips bacon

2 tsp olive oil

4 eggs

Black pepper

**ASSEMBLY**  Preheat oven to 375°F. Evenly coat a 9-inch square baking pan with cooking spray.

Bring a stockpot of salted water to a boil over high heat. Add pasta sheets and parboil according to the package's instructions. Drain, then rinse pasta under cold running water. Lay flat on a dish towel and pat-dry.

Add ¼ cup sausage ragu to the bottom of the prepared pan and spread out evenly. Top with 1 pasta sheet. Using a rubber spatula, spread ⅓ cup béchamel evenly on top of the pasta sheet. Top with another ¼ cup ragu.

Dollop 3 tablespoons of ricotta on top and sprinkle over 1½ tablespoons of Parmesan. Top with ¼ cup mozzarella. Top with 1 pasta sheet. Repeat, layering béchamel, ragu, ricotta, Parmesan, and mozzarella to make 10 layers.

Tightly cover with plastic wrap, followed by aluminum foil. Bake for 35–40 minutes, until bubbling. Carefully remove plastic and foil. Bake for another 5 minutes, until the top is golden brown. Set aside to rest for at least 15 minutes.

Heat a 10-inch skillet over medium heat. Add bacon and cook for 3 minutes on each side. Transfer to a paper towel–lined plate. Cool slightly, then chop to create a crumble.

Meanwhile, heat oil in an 8-inch skillet over medium heat. Add eggs and fry for 2½ minutes for sunny-side-up (or to your desired doneness). Season with salt and pepper.

Place a portion of lasagna on each plate, then top each serving with an egg and bacon. Spoon remaining béchamel, warmed, over top. Garnish with Parmesan.

p. 146

*Ten-Layer*
# BREAKFAST LASAGNA

# "Biscuits and Gravy" YORKSHIRE PUDDINGS

This recipe was inspired by a classic Southern breakfast combo, but this version doesn't actually have any biscuits. Instead, I've used Yorkshire puddings.

Similar to popovers, light and crispy Yorkshire puddings are traditionally served as part of a Sunday roast lunch in Britain. They make a delicious accompaniment to main dishes—or better yet, smother them with sausage gravy like I've done here.

## YORKSHIRE PUDDINGS

Cooking spray
1 cup + 2 Tbsp all-purpose
 flour
1 tsp kosher salt
4 eggs
¾ cup + 1 tsp whole milk

## SAUSAGE GRAVY

1 lb ground Italian sausage
1 cup (2 sticks) butter
1 cup all-purpose flour
2½ cups heavy cream
4 cups whole milk
1 tsp kosher salt
½ tsp black pepper
½ tsp smoked paprika
½ tsp garlic powder
¼ tsp onion powder

## ASSEMBLY

1 Tbsp olive oil
6 eggs
Kosher salt and black pepper
6 Yorkshire Puddings
 (see here), warmed
Sausage Gravy (see here)
Finely chopped chives, for garnish

**YORKSHIRE PUDDINGS**  Preheat oven to 445°F. Spray a muffin pan (or large cast-iron skillet) with cooking spray. Place in the oven for 5 minutes.

In a medium bowl, combine flour, salt, and eggs. Slowly whisk in milk until smooth. Transfer the batter to a measuring cup or jug for easy pouring. Fill muffin cups (or skillet) to three-quarters full. Place back in the oven for 10 minutes, until a toothpick comes out clean. (If using a skillet, let baked dough cool before cutting into six pieces.)

Makes 6 puddings. The batter is best used immediately, but it can be stored in the fridge for up to 4 hours.

**SAUSAGE GRAVY**  Heat a large saucepan over medium heat. Add sausage and sauté for 5–10 minutes, until browned. Using a slotted spoon, transfer sausage to a plate. Reserve the remaining fat in the pan.

Melt butter in a heavy saucepan over medium heat. Slowly add flour, whisking constantly, until the roux is lightly golden and smells like popcorn. Do not brown. Set aside.

Meanwhile, combine cream and milk in a separate large saucepan. Heat over medium heat until just before the mixture begins to boil. Slowly pour the hot milk mixture into the pan of roux, whisking continuously until smooth. Reduce heat to low, then add sausage and spices. Simmer for 10–15 minutes, until the mixture has thickened to a gravy.

**ASSEMBLY**  Heat oil in a 10-inch skillet over medium heat. Add eggs and fry for 2½ minutes for sunny-side-up (or to your desired doneness). Season with salt and pepper.

To serve, divide the Yorkshire puddings between two plates. Top each with an egg and gravy. Garnish with chives. Serve immediately.

# BRUNCH BURGER

SERVES 2

NF

If I put a burger on a menu, it has to be the best burger I have ever eaten. Here, I have a half-pound beef and bacon patty stacked with crispy hash browns, Pepper Jack cheese, fried onions, hollandaise, and a fried egg with an oozy yolk—and every bite pops. Pair this with one of my Bloody Marys (page 20) for the perfect hangover cure.

## HASH BROWNS

4 russet potatoes

2 eggs, beaten

1 large white onion, finely chopped

½ cup all-purpose flour

Kosher salt and black pepper, to taste

1–2 Tbsp canola oil

## BRUNCH BURGER

8 oz ground beef (90% lean)

8 oz bacon, finely chopped, + 4 strips cooked bacon

1 Tbsp butter

2 brioche burger buns

2 tsp olive or canola oil

2 eggs

Kosher salt and black pepper

2 slices Pepper Jack cheese

2 Hash Browns (see here)

½ cup Chef Pierce Hollandaise (page 169)

1 cup Fried Onions (page 109 [Carnitas Hash])

**HASH BROWNS** Shred potatoes with a box grater. Place in a medium bowl of ice water for 15 minutes. Drain, then rinse under cold running water until water runs clear. (This helps to remove excess starch.) Drain and squeeze dry.

In a large bowl, combine potatoes, eggs, onion, and flour. Season with salt and pepper and mix well.

Heat a large skillet over medium-high heat. Meanwhile, shape the potato mixture into golf-ball-sized balls. Flatten, then place on a paper towel–lined plate to drain excess moisture.

Add oil to the skillet. Carefully place potatoes in the hot oil and fry for 2–3 minutes on each side, until golden brown. For crispier hash browns, press down with a spatula after flipping. Transfer to a paper towel–lined plate to drain excess oil.

Hash browns can be stored in an airtight container and frozen for up to 3 months. To reheat, defrost at room temperature on a paper towel–lined plate.

**BRUNCH BURGER** Preheat oven to 350°F.

In a large bowl, combine ground beef and 8 ounces of bacon and mix thoroughly. Form into two patties.

Melt butter in a 10-inch skillet over medium heat. Add burger buns, cut sides down. Toast for 2–3 minutes, until golden brown. Set aside and cover with paper towels to keep warm.

Heat oil in a small skillet over medium heat. Add eggs, then break the yolks and cook for 2 minutes on each side, until the whites are set. Season with salt and pepper.

Heat a large ovenproof skillet over medium heat. Generously season both sides of the patties with salt and pepper. Cook for 3 minutes. Flip, then cook for another 3 minutes. Place in the oven and cook for another 4 minutes for medium.

Top with cheese and return to the oven for another minute, until cheese has melted.

Top each bottom bun with a hash brown, followed by a burger patty and egg. Pour hollandaise over top. Top with fried onions, two slices of bacon, and top bun.

Birria **BREAKFAST BURRITO** P. 157

# *Birria*
# BREAKFAST BURRITO

**SERVES 2**

**NF**

Everyone loves a breakfast burrito. We've rolled up crispy hash browns with birria, cheese, eggs, and salsa—and it's to die for.

5 tsp olive oil (divided)
2 Hash Browns (page 152 [Brunch Burger])
2 cups Birria (page 141)
4 eggs
Kosher salt and black pepper
2 (14-inch) flour tortillas
1 cup shredded mozzarella
½ cup Salsa Verde (page 166)

Heat 1 tablespoon of oil in a 10-inch skillet over medium-high heat. Add hash brown patties and pan-fry for 2 minutes on each side, until warmed through and crispy. Keep warm (such as uncovered in the microwave).

Heat birria in the same hot skillet for 3–5 minutes, until warmed through. Transfer to a serving plate and keep warm.

In a small bowl, whisk eggs. Season with salt and pepper.

Heat the remaining 2 teaspoons of oil in a sauté pan over medium heat. Pour in whisked eggs and stir constantly for 2–3 minutes (or to your desired doneness). Keep warm.

Meanwhile, heat a large skillet over medium heat. Add tortillas and warm for 1–1½ minutes, until they begin to color and start to bubble. Flip and cook for another minute, until warmed but still pliable.

Place each tortilla on a plate and add hash browns in the center of each tortilla. Top with birria, mozzarella, eggs, and salsa. Roll into a burrito by bringing the bottom of the tortilla up over the ingredients and pulling back towards you, allowing the ingredients to roll together. Tuck both edges in, facing the center, and roll away from you until tight.

Place burrito seam side down in the same large skillet over medium-high heat. Cook for 1½ minutes on each side, until burrito is sealed and golden brown.

# CROQUE MADAME SANDWICH

This is my favorite sandwich ever—how crazy is that? When I was thirteen, I was in Little Italy in New York with my uncle Arthur. I told him I was starving and wanted a panino, so he took me "for the best sandwich."

Thirty minutes later, we were in a French restaurant in midtown. I took one bite of the croque madame and asked, What the hell just happened to me?! Can I come every day? Now, I make this sandwich all the time at home and at the restaurants.

1 cup Béchamel (divided, page 146 [Ten-Layer Breakfast Lasagna])
4 slices brioche bread, 2 inches thick
2 Tbsp Dijon mustard
4 thin slices Black Forest ham
2 thin slices Gruyere
4 Tbsp butter
1 tsp olive or canola oil
2 eggs
Kosher salt and black pepper
2 Tbsp thinly sliced chives, for garnish
Grated Parmesan, for garnish

Preheat oven to 350°F.

Heat béchamel in a small saucepan over low heat until warmed through, stirring often to prevent scorching. Remove from heat and keep warm.

Lay out 2 slices of brioche. Spread each with 1 tablespoon of mustard, followed by ¼ cup béchamel. To each, add 2 slices of ham and 1 slice of cheese, which should slightly overlap the edges of the brioche. Top each with another brioche slice.

Melt butter in an ovenproof skillet over medium heat. Brush both sides of the sandwiches with melted butter, making sure that the edges are well covered. Toast sandwiches for 2 minutes on each side, until golden brown. Transfer the skillet to the oven and bake for 2–3 minutes, until heated through and cheese is bubbling.

Meanwhile, heat oil in an 8-inch skillet over medium heat. Add eggs and fry for 2½ minutes for sunny-side-up (or to your desired doneness). Season with salt and pepper and keep warm.

To serve, top each sandwich with a fried egg and remaining béchamel. Garnish with chives and grated Parmesan.

# *Birria*
# BRUNCH RAMEN

**SERVES 2**

**NF**

Ramen from an Italian chef? Why not! It's a hot item and delicious. I use less broth, so it's more of a noodle dish. With the birria and creamy Sriracha hollandaise, it's incredible.

## SRIRACHA HOLLANDAISE

6 egg yolks

1 Tbsp fresh lime juice

1 Tbsp Sriracha

1 cup (2 sticks) butter, melted and kept warm

Kosher salt, to taste

## RAMEN

10 oz ramen noodles (such as Sun Noodle Kaedama Ramen)

2 cups Birria (page 141)

1 cup Consommé (page 141)

2 tsp olive oil

4 eggs

Kosher salt and black pepper

1 lime, halved, for garnish

½ tsp Tajín

1 white onion, diced

1 cup Sriracha Hollandaise (see here)

½ cup thinly sliced scallions, for garnish

½ cup loosely packed cilantro leaves, for garnish

**SRIRACHA HOLLANDAISE** Place egg yolks, lime juice, and Sriracha in a blender. Blend on high speed for 30 seconds, whipping air into the mixture.

With the motor still running, slowly pour butter in a thin and steady stream and blend until smooth and creamy. Season with salt. Makes 1 cup. Use immediately.

**RAMEN** Cook ramen according to the package's instructions. Strain in a mesh food strainer and rinse with cold water to remove excess starch.

Combine birria and consommé in a 10-inch skillet and warm for 5 minutes over medium heat, until heated through. Using a slotted spoon, transfer birria to a dish. Leave consommé in the skillet and keep both warm.

Meanwhile, heat oil in an 8-inch skillet over medium heat. Add eggs and fry for 2½ minutes for sunny-side-up (or to your desired doneness). Season with salt and pepper. Keep warm.

Toss noodles in consommé to coat and warm through.

Dip lime in Tajín.

To serve, evenly divide noodles between two bowls. Place half the birria on one side of each bowl. Top each with onion and 2 eggs. Drizzle with hollandaise, and garnish with scallions, cilantro, and lime.

# THERE'S PLENTY HERE

to take your brunch game to a whole new level. The recipes in this chapter are fantastic components to the fun, over-the-top recipes in this book, but you could easily serve them alongside your favorite dishes, as well. Slather that salsa verde on fried chicken bao buns or create your own killer biscuit combinations. Who knows what might happen, but I guarantee that your successes will take your weekend parties to new heights.

Note that when baking, we prefer to measure ingredients by weight instead of volume for precision and a consistent result.

# BACK TO BASICS

# SALSA ROJO

**MAKES ABOUT 1 CUP**

DF  NF

Guajillo peppers are dried, dark-red, medium-sized chiles. Known for their rich, fruity flavor and moderate spice, they need to be reconstituted before being blended into salsas. Whole guajillo peppers can be found in grocery stores, Mexican markets, and online shops. (Alternatively, look for dried ancho chiles, which may be easier to find.)

1 oz dried guajillo peppers, stemmed and seeded
½ Tbsp olive oil
¼ white onion, sliced
½ garlic clove, finely chopped
½ Tbsp chicken base powder
¾ tsp kosher salt
Pinch of paprika
Pinch of chili powder
Pinch of black pepper

Place guajillo peppers in a large saucepan and cover with water. Bring to a boil and boil for 15 minutes. Drain, reserving ½ cup water. Set aside to cool.

Add peppers and reserved water to a blender and blend until smooth.

Heat oil in the same saucepan over medium heat. Add onion and sauté for 5–7 minutes, until translucent. Add the guajillo pepper purée and remaining ingredients. Bring to a boil, then remove from heat and allow to cool.

Salsa can be stored in the fridge for up to 4 days.

# SALSA VERDE

Native to Central America, tomatillos resemble small green tomatoes encased in papery husks. Look for firm, plump, bright green fruit. You'll need to remove the husks and rinse the tomatillos to remove any residue or stickiness. When raw, they are firm and crisp with a bright, acidic taste. Cooked tomatillos become softer and milder in flavor.

1 serrano pepper, stemmed
6 firm tomatillos, husked
 and washed (about 2 lbs)
½ Tbsp olive oil
¼ white onion, finely chopped
2 garlic cloves, finely chopped
2 Tbsp chicken base powder
¼ tsp kosher salt
Pinch of black pepper
Pinch of granulated sugar

Place serrano pepper and tomatillos in a medium saucepan. Add enough water to cover them. Bring to a boil, reduce heat to medium-low, and simmer for 10 minutes. Drain, then set aside to cool.

Transfer the tomatillo mixture to a blender and blend until smooth.

Heat oil in a medium saucepan over medium heat. Add onion and sauté for 7 minutes, until softened and translucent. Add garlic, chicken base, the tomatillo mixture, and ¼ cup water. Bring to a boil. Season with salt, pepper, and sugar. Set aside to cool.

Salsa can be stored in an airtight container in the fridge for up to 4 days.

SALSA
ROJO
P.165

SALSA
VERDE
P.166

# THE CHEF PIERCE HOLLANDAISE, *Blender Version*

**MAKES ABOUT 1 CUP**

VEG · GF · NF

Hollandaise sauce is a rich, buttery sauce traditionally made by whisking ingredients over gentle heat. An essential for eggs Benedict, this shortcut version is made in a blender and the perfect addition to your culinary arsenal.

6 egg yolks
2 Tbsp lemon juice
1 tsp hot sauce (such as Valentina Salsa Picante)
⅛ tsp paprika
1 cup (2 sticks) butter, melted and warm
Kosher salt, to taste

Place egg yolks, lemon juice, hot sauce, and paprika in a blender. Blend on high speed for 30 seconds, whipping air into the mixture.

With the motor still running, slowly pour in butter in a thin and steady stream until the mixture is creamy and smooth. Season with salt. Use immediately.

# GREEN CHILE HOLLANDAISE, *Blender Version*

**MAKES 2 CUPS**

**NF**

Adding spicy-tangy salsa verde to classic hollandaise is a Southwestern twist guaranteed to up your brunch game. Try adding this sauce to any brunch dish you want to transform into a Mexican fiesta, from breakfast burritos to Benedicts.

6 egg yolks

2 Tbsp lemon juice

⅛ tsp paprika

1 tsp hot sauce (such as Valentina Salsa Picante)

1 cup (2 sticks) butter, melted and warm

½ cup Salsa Verde (page 166)

Kosher salt, to taste

Place egg yolks, lemon juice, paprika, and hot sauce in a blender. Blend on high speed for 30 seconds, whipping air into the mixture.

With the motor still running, slowly pour in butter in a thin and steady stream until the mixture is creamy and smooth. Add salsa. Blend for 20 more seconds, until incorporated. Season with salt. Use immediately.

# CANNOLI CREAM

**MAKES 2½ CUPS**

VEG  GF  NF

Vanilla-scented ricotta with a hint of lemon zest and a sprinkle of chocolate chips—this cream is so good you might start to have an Italian accent. Whether you're stuffing it into donuts (page 39) or slathering it on pancakes (page 60), this cream will add my Italian flair to any sweet brunch dish.

2½ cups whole milk ricotta (such as Polly-O)
2 cups confectioners' sugar
¾ tsp vanilla extract
⅛ tsp ground cinnamon
1 tsp grated lemon zest
½ cup semisweet chocolate chips

Place ricotta in a fine-mesh strainer set over a medium bowl. Cover and store in the fridge for 12 hours or overnight to drain excess moisture.

Place drained ricotta in a large bowl, then add the remaining ingredients. Mix thoroughly until smooth and combined.

Store in the fridge in a piping bag or zip-top bag for up to 4 days.

# CRÈME BRÛLÉE CUSTARD

**MAKES 1¾ CUPS**

VEG · GF · NF

As a young chef, I thought it would be cool to make crème brûlée in the restaurant. My dad said, "What the heck? That's French! Make panna cotta instead!"

I discovered it was such an easy dessert to make—and you can use the custard for so many things.

4 egg yolks
¼ cup granulated sugar
1¾ cups heavy cream
1 Madagascar vanilla bean,
　split lengthwise

Fill a medium saucepan halfway with water. Bring to a simmer over medium-high heat.

Meanwhile, whisk egg yolks and sugar in a heatproof bowl large enough to fit over the pan. Whisk until smooth and pale yellow. Set aside.

Pour cream into a small saucepan. With the tip of a knife, scrape seeds from the vanilla bean into the pan, add bean, and stir. Bring to a simmer over medium-high heat, making sure not to burn the mixture. Simmer gently for 3 minutes. Remove bean and scrape any more seeds into the pan. Stir and simmer for 3 more minutes.

Ladle a small amount of cream into the egg mixture, whisking continuously. (This tempers the eggs. If hot cream is added at once, the eggs will scramble.) Keep adding ladles of cream, whisking continuously, until incorporated.

Place the bowl over the saucepan of simmering water and whisk vigorously, occasionally scraping the sides to prevent eggs from scrambling. Whisk until the mixture forms a smooth custard. Remove from heat, then transfer to a container (or spread in a baking pan to cool faster).

Store in the fridge for up to 3 days or freeze for up to 1 month. If using frozen custard, defrost in the fridge for 2 days.

# BUTTERMILK BISCUITS

**MAKES 12**

**VEG** **NF**

The flakiest biscuits are formed when pockets of butter are steamed in the oven and create airy layers. The trick is to use very cold buttermilk and frozen butter to prevent the butter in the dough from melting before it hits the oven. You'll also want to work quickly to keep the dough as chilled and underworked as possible.

Cooking spray
3¾ cups (465 g) self-rising flour (such as White Lily), plus extra for dusting
1 Tbsp (15 g) baking powder
1½ Tbsp (19 g) granulated sugar
1 tsp (5 g) kosher salt
¾ cup (170 g) frozen salted butter
1½ cups (368 g) very cold buttermilk
2 eggs (100 g)

Preheat oven to 400°F. Line a baking sheet with parchment paper and coat with cooking spray.

Sift flour, baking powder, sugar, and salt into a medium bowl. Whisk to combine.

Using a box grater, grate butter into the bowl. Using your fingers, quickly mix into pea-sized crumbs. Pour in buttermilk and mix with your hands until the dough just comes together. It will be slightly wet.

Lightly flour the dough and press it into a ball, then place it on a lightly floured surface. Using a rolling pin, roll out the dough to between ¾–1-inch thick. (The thickness will determine the fluffiness of the biscuits.) With a ring mold or biscuit cutter, cut out 3-inch round biscuits. Arrange them on the prepared baking sheet.

In a small bowl, whisk eggs and 1¾ fl oz water. Brush the tops of the biscuits with the egg mixture. Bake for 7 minutes. Rotate the pan, then bake for another 7–8 minutes, until the biscuits are golden brown.

# BAO BUNS

MAKES
12

VEG  NF

Bao buns are also known as "Chinese steam buns." Soft and puffy, they make the perfect vehicle for a variety of fillings, such as Birria (page 141).

If you don't own a bamboo steamer, use a flat strainer, vegetable steamer, or metal colander lined with parchment paper set in a large saucepan. Be sure the water doesn't touch the steamer and that the saucepan has a tight-fitting lid.

3 Tbsp (43 g) butter
⅔ cup + 1 Tbsp (178 g)
  lukewarm whole milk
2½ tsp (7 g) active dry yeast
2¾ cups (330 g) bread flour
  (preferably King Arthur)
2¾ Tbsp (35 g) granulated sugar
1 tsp (5 g) kosher salt
½ tsp (2 g) baking powder
½ tsp (2 g) baking soda
Cooking spray

Heat butter in the microwave until just melted. Do not allow it to get too hot, as a temperature over 115°F will kill the yeast.

In a large bowl, whisk butter, milk, and yeast until yeast is dissolved.

Into a separate medium bowl, sift flour, sugar, salt, baking powder, and baking soda. Whisk to combine. Add the dry mixture to the wet mixture, ½ cup at a time, and whisk until combined. Knead to form a soft dough. (Alternatively, use a stand mixer fitted with the hook attachment and mix on low speed.) Knead for another 5–10 minutes, until the dough has come together and no longer sticks to the sides of the bowl.

Remove the dough from the bowl, form into a ball, and set aside. Lightly grease the bottom of a large bowl with cooking spray, place the dough in the bowl, and cover with plastic wrap. Allow the dough to rise at room temperature until it doubles in size (about 1 hour depending on kitchen temperature).

Place the dough onto a clean work surface. Using a rolling pin, roll out the dough to about ¼-inch thick. Using a 3-inch ring mold, cut out 12 buns. Lightly spray buns with cooking spray, then fold them into half-moons.

Bring a wok or large saucepan of water to a boil over medium-high heat. Line a steamer with parchment paper. Arrange buns in the steamer and carefully place them over the boiling water (do not allow buns to touch the water). Cover and steam for 6–8 minutes, until puffed. Transfer to a baking sheet lined with parchment paper and cover with plastic wrap or a dish towel until ready to serve.

Steamed buns can be frozen for up to 3 months. To reheat, thaw for 15 minutes at room temperature, then steam again for 4–5 minutes or warm in the microwave.

# SMOKED BRISKET

No smoker? No problem! For a shortcut for those without a barbecue rig, get that tender texture and smoky flavor with a long, slow oven braise, a dash of liquid smoke, and my killer brisket rub.

### SPICE RUB
1½ Tbsp kosher salt
1½ Tbsp brown sugar
1½ Tbsp dried thyme
2½ tsp chili powder
2½ tsp paprika
2½ tsp dried mustard
2½ tsp garlic powder
2½ tsp onion powder

### SMOKED BRISKET
4 lbs boneless beef brisket
Spice Rub (see here)
2 Tbsp liquid smoke

**SPICE RUB** Combine all ingredients in a small bowl and mix well.

**SMOKED BRISKET** Preheat oven to 250°F.

Using a sharp knife, carefully trim off the hard fat from the brisket. Evenly coat brisket with spice rub.

Set a wire roasting rack in a large roasting pan. Pour in 3 cups water and add liquid smoke. Insert an oven-safe thermometer into the thickest part of the brisket and place brisket on the wire roasting rack. If necessary, remove enough water so that brisket does not touch water. Cover with aluminum foil, ensuring the thermometer is visible. Slow-roast for 5½ hours, until the internal temperature reaches 175°F. Remove the foil and cook for 1½ hours, until the internal temperature reaches 195°F.

Remove pan from oven, cover, and set aside to rest for at least 30 minutes. Slice against the grain for optimal tenderness.

# METRIC CONVERSION CHART

## VOLUME

IMPERIAL OR U.S. → METRIC

⅛ tsp → 0.5 mL
¼ tsp → 1 mL
½ tsp → 2.5 mL
¾ tsp → 4 mL
1 tsp → 5 mL
1½ tsp → 8 mL
1 Tbsp → 15 mL
1½ Tbsp → 23 mL
2 Tbsp → 30 mL
¼ cup → 60 mL
⅓ cup → 80 mL
½ cup → 125 mL
⅔ cup → 165 mL
¾ cup → 185 mL
1 cup → 250 mL
1¼ cups → 310 mL
1⅓ cups → 330 mL
1½ cups → 375 mL
1⅔ cups → 415 mL
1¾ cups → 435 mL
2 cups → 500 mL
2¼ cups → 560 mL
2⅓ cups → 580 mL
2½ cups → 625 mL
2¾ cups → 690 mL
3 cups → 750 mL
4 cups / 1 quart → 1 L
5 cups → 1.25 L
6 cups → 1.5 L
7 cups → 1.75 L
8 cups → 2 L
12 cups → 3 L

## LIQUID MEASURES (FOR ALCOHOL)

IMPERIAL OR U.S. → METRIC

½ fl oz → 15 mL
1 fl oz → 30 mL
2 fl oz → 60 mL
3 fl oz → 90 mL
4 fl oz → 120 mL

## CANS AND JARS

IMPERIAL OR U.S. → METRIC

6 oz → 170 mL
14 oz → 398 mL
19 oz → 540 mL
28 oz → 796 mL

## WEIGHT

IMPERIAL OR U.S. → METRIC

½ oz → 15 g
1 oz → 30 g
2 oz → 60 g
3 oz → 85 g
4 oz (¼ lb) → 115 g
5 oz → 140 g
6 oz → 170 g
7 oz → 200 g
8 oz (½ lb) → 225 g
9 oz → 255 g
10 oz → 285 g
11 oz → 310 g
12 oz (¾ lb) → 340 g
13 oz → 370 g
14 oz → 400 g
15 oz → 425 g
16 oz (1 lb) → 450 g
1¼ lbs → 570 g
1½ lbs → 670 g
2 lbs → 900 g
3 lbs → 1.4 kg
4 lbs → 1.8 kg
5 lbs → 2.3 kg
6 lbs → 2.7 kg

## LINEAR

IMPERIAL OR U.S. → METRIC

⅛ inch → 3 mm

¼ inch → 6 mm

½ inch → 12 mm

¾ inch → 2 cm

1 inch → 2.5 cm

1¼ inches → 3 cm

1½ inches → 3.5 cm

1¾ inches → 4.5 cm

2 inches → 5 cm

2½ inches → 6.5 cm

3 inches → 7.5 cm

4 inches → 10 cm

5 inches → 12.5 cm

6 inches → 15 cm

7 inches → 18 cm

10 inches → 25 cm

12 inches (1 foot) → 30 cm

13 inches → 33 cm

16 inches → 41 cm

18 inches → 46 cm

24 inches (2 feet) → 60 cm

28 inches → 70 cm

30 inches → 75 cm

6 feet → 1.8 m

## TEMPERATURE

(for oven temperatures,
see chart in next column)

IMPERIAL OR U.S. → METRIC

90°F → 32°C

120°F → 49°C

125°F → 52°C

130°F → 54°C

140°F → 60°C

150°F → 66°C

155°F → 68°C

160°F → 71°C

165°F → 74°C

170°F → 77°C

175°F → 80°C

180°F → 82°C

190°F → 88°C

200°F → 93°C

240°F → 116°C

250°F → 121°C

300°F → 149°C

325°F → 163°C

350°F → 177°C

360°F → 182°C

375°F → 191°C

## OVEN TEMPERATURE

IMPERIAL OR U.S. → METRIC

200°F → 95°C

250°F → 120°C

275°F → 135°C

300°F → 150°C

325°F → 160°C

350°F → 180°C

375°F → 190°C

400°F → 200°C

425°F → 220°C

450°F → 230°C

500°F → 260°C

550°F → 290°C

## BAKING PANS

IMPERIAL OR U.S. → METRIC

5- × 9-inch loaf pan → 2 L loaf pan

9- × 13-inch cake pan → 4 L cake pan

11- × 17-inch → 30- × 45-cm
baking sheet       baking sheet

# INDEX

bruschetta, crème brûlée, *42, 43*
buns, bao, 176
    for birria bao Benedict, 93
burger, brunch, 152, *153*
burrito, birria breakfast, 157, *154–56*
butter, salted honey, 59
BUTTERMILK
    biscuit dough, in that funky
        monkey bread, 40
    biscuits, 175
    biscuits, in fried chicken
        Benedict, 86
    -brined chicken, 134
    in carrot cake pancakes with
        cream cheese icing, 64
    in fried onions, 109
    pancake batter, in cannoli
        pancakes, 60
    pancakes, better-than-your-mama's
        malted, 59

C

CANNOLI
    cream, 172, *173*
    donuts, *38, 39*
    pancakes, 60, *61*
capers, in smoked salmon frittata,
    105
caramel, salted (drink), *28*, 30
caramel sauce, in banana split
    French toast, 48–49
carbonara hash, gnocchi, *120*, 121–22
carne asada, 118
carnitas, 139
    in Cristina's tamale cakes Benedict,
        89–90
    hash, 109, *110*
    in hash avocado toast, 135
CARROT
    in braised short ribs, 138
    cake pancakes with cream cheese
        icing, 64, *65*
    in sausage ragu, 146
CAYENNE
    in blackening seasoning, 127
    in chicken flour, for fried chicken,
        134
celery salt, in Bloody Mary mixes,
    20
CEREAL
    Cocoa Krispies, in cocoa crispies
        (drink), 34
    Fruity Pebbles, in Fruity Pebbles
        treats, 35
    Fruity Pebbles, in the bedrock
        (drink), 35

CHALLAH BREAD
    in banana split French toast,
        48–49
    in bread pudding French toast
        sticks, 53–54
    in classic French toast, 45
    in s'mores French toast, 50
cheddar, in potato skin Benedict, 85
CHEESE. *See also* Cotija cheese;
                cream cheese; mascarpone;
                mozzarella; Parmesan;
                ricotta
    cheddar, in potato skin Benedict,
        85
    cottage, in bling bling blintzes, 73
    Gruyere, in croque madame
        sandwich, 159
    Pepper Jack, in brunch burger,
        152
    provolone, in zucchini, potato,
        and onion frittata, 96
Chef Joey's Bloody Mary mix, 20
the Chef Pierce hollandaise, *168, 169*
    in best f#*%ing birria hash, 117
    in birria bao Benedict, 93
    in brunch burger, 152
    in fried chicken Benedict, 86
    in potato skin Benedict, 85
    in smoked brisket and cornbread
        hash, 115
CHERRIES, AMARENA
    in cannoli donuts, 39
    in cannoli pancakes, 60
CHICKEN. *See also* chicken stock
    fried, 134
    fried, and waffles, *78–79*, 80
    fried, Benedict, 86, *87*
    tinga, in chilaquiles, 143
    tinga, in tinga frittata, 103
CHICKEN STOCK
    in braised short ribs, 138
    in brown demi gravy, 112
    in carnitas, 139
    in mascarpone polenta, 127
chilaquiles, *142*, 143
CHILES. *See* chipotle; guajillo pepper;
                Morita chiles, in tinga;
                mulato pepper, in birria and
                consommé; serrano pepper,
                in salsa verde
chili flakes, in chili–brown sugar rub,
    133
CHILI POWDER
    in salsa rojo, 165
    in spice rub, for smoked brisket, 177

CHIPOTLE
    -Habanero Bloody Mary Seasoning,
        in too hott!!! Bloody Mary
        mix, 20
    peppers in adobo, in tinga, 143
CHIVES
    in "biscuits and gravy" Yorkshire
        puddings, 150
    in blackened shrimp and grits hash,
        128
    in blue crab and sweet potato hash,
        124
    in croque madame sandwich,
        159
    in fried chicken Benedict, 86
    in short rib poutine hash, 112
    in smoked brisket and cornbread
        hash, 115
    in smoked salmon frittata, 105
CHOCOLATE. *See also*
                chocolate syrup
    chips, in cannoli cream, 172
    chips, in cannoli pancakes, 60
    in Italian espresso martini, 30
    in s'more (drink), 31
CHOCOLATE SYRUP
    in cocoa crispies (drink), 34
    in s'more (drink), 31
    in tiramisu (drink), 31
chuck roast, in birria and consommé,
    141
CILANTRO
    in best f#*%ing birria hash, 117
    in birria bao Benedict, 93
    in birria brunch ramen, 160
    in carnitas hash, 109
    in chilaquiles, 143
    in Cristina's tamale cakes Benedict,
        90
    in huevos rancheros hash, 118
    in Maso's breakfast potato tacos,
        145
    in tinga frittata, 103
CINNAMON
    in better-than-your-mama's malted
        buttermilk pancakes, 59
    in birria and consommé, 141
    in blue corn bananas Foster
        pancakes, 62
    in bread pudding French toast
        sticks, 53–54
    in cannoli cream, 172
    in cannoli pancakes, 60
    in carrot cake pancakes with cream
        cheese icing, 64

# ACKNOWLEDGMENTS

This incredible book could not have become a reality without the help of the following amazing humans:

To my father, Chef Tomaso, for passing on your passion and talent in the kitchen to me. Without you, I would never have become the chef and restaurateur I am today and, most importantly, a great man. Your legacy and memories will always guide me, and I hope I have made you proud.

To my beautiful mom, Patricia, for your unconditional love and always pushing me to be the best chef and person I can be. And yes, you deserve the credit for encouraging me to open a brunch concept— I will never forget that.

To my sister, Melissa, for always standing by me, supporting my ideas, and encouraging me to be the best.

To my amazing, hot wife, Cristina, for never giving up on me and my dreams and for sacrificing so much for so many years. Your hard work and dedication are mind blowing, and I will always be in awe of your beauty, work ethic, and talent in designing our restaurants' décor. Thank you for always pushing me to be a great dad and husband. I could never have done this without you, and you will always be my true love. Thank you for giving me the greatest gift of my life, our children.

To my children, Giuliana, Tomaso, and Melina: I love you all more than life itself and admire what amazing humans you have become. I love being your papa, and I can't wait to see how you will leave your mark on this world.

To Seth Widdes: Thank you for your dedication in keeping me focused and on track and for your great ideas. Your contribution helped elevate this beyond an average cookbook.

To Chef Pierce Azlin: Thank you for helping to organize and execute my amazing recipes. I know that was a huge task. Your culinary talent really shines through, especially with the carrot cake pancakes. Ha!

To Chef Thierry Delourneaux: Thank you for sharing your talent, dealing with our crazy R & D, and producing some of the best pastries and pancakes. You truly are an artist.

To Christina Barrueta: Thank you for your writing talent. You're an amazing writer and the best culinary storyteller I have ever met. This book would not have been as good without your hard work and dedication. Thank you for being a part of something truly special.

To my partners, Tony and Flora Tersigni, for believing in my crazy ideas and supporting me. Most importantly, thank you for your friendship and love.

To Chef Rigo Martinez for helping make the magic for this book.

To Joanie Simon, the best food photographer there is, for making my food stand out like me.

To the Savory Restaurant Fund, Andrew and Shauna Smith, for believing in the Hash Kitchen brand and helping us transform our brunch concept into a household name.

# ABOUT THE AUTHOR

Combining his Sicilian heritage with modern culinary techniques, chef and restaurateur Joey Maggiore, known better as "Chef Joey," is the entrepreneur behind Chef Joey Concepts and The Maggiore Group. With his wife, Cristina, he has founded the award-winning restaurant concepts Hash Kitchen, The Sicilian Butcher, The Sicilian Baker, The Mexicano, The Rosticceria, The Italiano, and Il Massetos. Known for creating extraordinary and unforgettable dining experiences, Chef Joey has been honored by The National Italian American Foundation for his culinary contributions and is the recipient of multiple Foodist awards, including Top Chef. His magnetic personality has also earned him appearances on popular television networks such as Food Network and Travel Channel. Chef Joey lives in Scottsdale, Arizona, with Cristina and their three children, Giuliana, Tomaso, and Melina.

in @chefjoeymaggiore

♪ @chefjoeymaggiore